The Soni<

DNA Activa

by Gary & JoAnn Chambers

The Sonic Keys: DNA Activation 101

Copyright © 2014 Gary & JoAnn Chambers

All rights reserved. No part of this book may be reproduced, stored, transmitted or otherwise copied without prior written permission of the publisher. Brief quotations and references may be used with appropriate credit lines.

The information in this book does not replace professional medical advice nor does it prescribe any treatment for any physical, mental or emotional illness or disease. The contents of this book is for adventurous explorers seeking to expand their consciousness by stepping beyond what is commonly considered "normal." This work is to be considered experimental and for those seeking adventures into multidimensional landscapes within the higher realms of Light & Sound. It is up to each individual engaging with this material to be responsible for his or her own welfare and the authors and publishers assume no responsibility for your interpretation of this material. Honor the work and respect the process.

Published by:
Visionary Music, Inc.
5400 Park Street N #105
St. Petersburg, FL 33709
727.235.6302
info@visionarymusic.com
VisionaryMusic.com

Available at ActivateYourDNA.com & Amazon.com

First Edition, January 2014

The Sonic Keys
Sound, Light & Frequency
DNA Activation 101

Contents

Preface • 4
Introduction • 4
DNA Activation 101 • 6
The Awakening & Activation • 11
Signs of Emergence • 16
Exploring the Potentials & Possibilities • 19
Engaged & Focused Listening • 22
DNA Strands as Metaphors • 27
The Unfolding Process • 28
Complementary Spiritual Work • 30
Convergence of Science & Spirituality • 31
Multidimensional Sound is the Sonic Key • 34
Harmonic Resonance in Action • 37
Spiritual Evolution • 40
A Lifetime of Empowerment • 42
A Greater Purpose • 44
Energetic Transmissions of Information • 46
Evolutionary Sounds • 48
For Spiritual Seekers • 51
Faith & Trust • 53
Things to Consider • 56
Sonic Mystery School • 59
Explorations with Other Soundscapes • 59
A Visual Journey • 62
About Us • 63
Closing • 64
Free MP3 Music Soundfile • 66

Preface

This is the 2nd book in The Sonic Key series, which focuses on the DNA Activation process using the multidimensional music created by Gary & JoAnn Chambers. It is suggested that you have at least one of the DNA Activation LevelOne soundscapes available to listen to as you start to read. For a greater understanding of the material presented here, we suggest you read the first book in this series titled *The Sonic Keys: Sound, Light & Frequency* first.

This book is written for beginners exploring the topic of DNA Activation, using our multidimensional music, to help you understand some of the basic and more complex principles of the process. If the material is challenging to you at first, we suggest you start with just listening to the music, letting yourself go into exploring the various sounds. Close your eyes and allow the music to open up new pathways of higher understanding, initiating the assimilation process of sonic-based information, allowing these concepts to go much deeper. The chapters in this book were taken from various Q&As and we compiled the important ones that were most appropriate for a beginners introduction. You may see some redundancy and some overlap, but we chose to leave them close to what these original responses were to maintain the flow of information within each chapter. We suggest that you reread this book or just certain chapters from time to time as you will gain more insights with each review.

Introduction

Welcome to our Sonic Mystery School. This is a grand adventure that few choose to travel; yet it is one that promises to engage you in wondrous and magical adventures for the rest of your life. If you are a seeker of truth who is looking to find more meaning in your Life on Planet Earth, then starting this path of DNA Activation is quite likely one of the secret keys you have been looking for.

What was Hidden, is now Revealed

The 3rd dimensional (3D) world in which we live, on the most basic levels, is a vast vibratory field – pure vital energy suspended in a dimension we call time. Anything that vibrates produces sound, whether the frequencies are audible or not; it is all sonic information. We live in a sea of sound. Our bodies are composed of various combinations of frequencies which give us our physical forms. Our DNA contains the blueprint that includes the instructions for your physical form to live and thrive in this 3D environment. It also contains the data needed to allow your spiritual form to inhabit and reside within the physical body. In addition to this fundamental survival level information, there are dormant codes within the DNA that wait for the individual Soul to reach a certain level of awareness to become active; this is the start of the awakened or enlightened state. We, Gary & JoAnn Chambers, create evolutionary sounds for the purpose of establishing a conscious communication link with our DNA to awaken these dormant codes. Once these codes awaken, it starts the process of activating the next levels of higher potentials available to humanity. This process of using sound is the most powerful DNA Activation process available for those who are serious about their path of Conscious Evolution.

Our approach to this work emanates primarily from the spiritual disciplines. In time, science will have the methods and the tools to break things down into the statistical data that would be required for factual proof. But our job at this time is to be explorers and adventurers in to what is possible using our consciousness directed by our focused intent, followed by tangible actions. It is not enough to engage the fantasy of the imagination without also connecting to the 3rd dimensional reality. We are intending full spectrum integration of the multidimensional being from the highest spiritual realms to the densest physical reality.

The Sonic Keys series focuses on teachings about the higher aspects of Sound and its potential and practical applications in your life. We invite you to journey along with us as we share the many nuances that can be explored within the multidimensional landscapes of our sonic transmissions. This work is for the adventurous spirit willing to bypass the traditional and known ways of our current cultural programming.

Within your DNA there are already codes that have awakened which tell you there is more to this existence than what is being presented as "living life on Planet Earth in the 21st century." You will know deep within your Soul that you have incarnated in this timeline to break free of your culture, your stereotype and your gender and move into the next phase of your human existence. The information in this book series is merely the tip of the proverbial iceberg. They will be future books to help you begin to navigate the multidimensional worlds of information we present to you in our various soundscapes. Within the music, we provide you with sonic information from the quantum levels of reality, from beyond where all mental constructs and intellectual bantering occurs. We call this Quantum Sonic Empowerment Technology or QSET.

Engage to the depth you are willing to embrace change in your life. This is for Spiritual Warriors who have arrived at that significant place in their Soul's journey when it is time to make the leap to the next level of existence, beyond the tick-tock world and into the magical realms of Unlimited Potentials.

Welcome to our adventures in Sound.

DNA Activation 101

The possibilities are endless when it comes to just what you can accomplish while consciously focusing on activating your DNA. As humanity has evolved, our primary focus has been placed on outward manifestations. We have built a magical world here on Planet Earth. Collectively we have designed it step by step – it is our agreed upon Reality Construct. If you want better eyesight, get glasses. If you want different hair color, you can dye it. If you are sick, get a pill. If you get wrinkles, get botox. If you are unhappy, take a vacation or take another pill! This list goes on and on, but basically we have shifted away from our innate personal power and mostly rely on things that are created in the 3D Reality Construct. While this is powerful magic on its own, because of so much external focus, we have lost our own inner abilities to create magic directly with our connection to Source Vibration. This is something we are fully capable of and each of us has this ability. This process of DNA Activation is just at the beginning stages of being understood, as well as what it takes in terms of development from the individual to bring forth these manifestations into our known reality. It is truly pioneering work that takes practice to really discover all the potentials we have yet to unfold. Each person engaged with this process chooses their particular area of focused desires and will work on it initially for themselves, but as they perfect the process it goes into the collective DNA and awakens these potentials in others. So only you can decide where this work can take you based on your personal desires and focus.

> *DNA Activation is a spiritually focused process of awakening dormant potentials within the multidimensional human DNA codex. Our Intention is to unlock these codes using our multidimensional music & sound.*

This book will be focusing on our unique approach to activating the DNA using our multidimensional sounds and music. This is a very personal spiritual journey, and so it must be understood on all levels of your being what that really means. You will know deep within that it is time for you to truly discover who you are and what you are capable of actualizing in this 3D realm of matter. You also know that above all, you are a spiritual being of Light inhabiting this physical existence for a period of time to evolve to your next higher level of manifestation – what we call the 5th World of Light or 5D (5th dimension).

We have been guided step by step in this work by our own personal journeys of inner explorations – teachings and lessons through the darkest of nights awakening into the brightest Light of day. DNA Activation is not an easy path to walk, but it is very rewarding for the Soul. It is not one that can promise you the road to success without hard work and dedication on your part – at least not in the traditional meanings of what success is considered to be for modern society. Shifting between living from your 3D-life to a spiritually focused 5D-life will be a continual challenge for you as you walk this path.

The results you can attain with DNA Activation go beyond the typical 3D skills and talents that one develops in creative pursuits, academics, athletics or business abilities. While it includes these attributes, it also requires full observation of one's ethics, integrity and honesty in all your dealings with others and the world. As you learn to live your life attuned to the world of energy, you clearly begin to understand how all your interactions with this field create the results of the life you are living. The cessation of karmic patterns ends here, through conscious awareness of all your interactions with the world around you. Whether one views karma from a science background based on the physics of actions and reactions or from the spiritual perspective of energetic patterns of reaping and sowing matters not. Either perspective is ultimately a mental construct we create to wrap our minds around a series of thoughts to help us try to comprehend something which is ultimately beyond all knowingness on those levels of awareness. The expansion of consciousness that is required to fully embrace this process takes time, dedication and much practice to fully understand the ramifications of what it means to assume a conscious role in the activation of your multi-strand DNA codex. It is a profound responsibility that you agree to take on and not something that is done in one healing session or a weekend workshop. The actual commitment is really a lifelong dedication to a deeper understanding of Life and your human and spiritual existence.

The process requires continual awareness of the levels of Light that you are operating from at all times; your Light Quotient. When intending to live from the Light side of the experiential spectrum of life, while knowingly or unknowingly still holding vibrations of a darker nature, you will continually experience life in disharmony with the world around you. The frequency patterns you are generating are always in conflict with each other. This results in the decreasing of your Light Quotient which bring forth thoughts and feelings of lack, limitation and lowered self-worth, which is in the frequency zones of depression, anxiety, addictions and destructive behaviors. This is the Lower Self Matrix that dominates one's life until you consciously choose to evolve – Conscious Evolution. When one chooses to walk a path of Conscious Evolution, he lives predominantly in alignment with his Higher Self Matrix.

Your DNA sends and receives messages constantly based on your environments and the emotional qualities that you engage within: people, places, events, situations, locations. It reacts to these messages, and the results can produce either positive or negative outcomes depending on the combination of the frequency patterns you are emitting as a result. The repeated grooves within these patterns call you back time and time again to repeat the same situations, which are the most difficult ones to change and step out of without upsetting the life that you are currently living. Your desire to change these patterns will affect those around you, as they may be unwilling to change in response. Serious time will be spent to determine your levels of responsibility to those around you and what you have already become deeply entangled in. Careful examination of one's previous life choices and how they have led to the current life you are living takes time to explore. Initially there is a deconstruction phase leading to a reconstruction phase, before the rebuilding phase can occur.

The DNA is a receiver and a transmitter.

We all have elements of dark and light within us. Most present their Light side to those around them while hiding their dark side in secrecy. This is not a path without some conscious engagement of your dark side, however, as it is required to access this darker nature and transform it to Light to be utilized for true empowerment. There is a tremendous amount of power and strength within this frequency band of energy. As long as it remains hidden, it creates problems throughout your life as it subtly sabotages your higher visions. The transformation of this is an alchemical process of transmutation. It is one of the deepest and most ancient forms of shapeshifting.

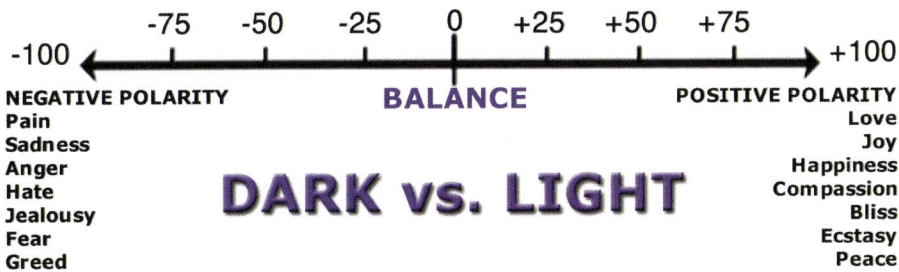

Figure 1. We each have all these traits within us to express and experience. Ultimately we learn to maintain a balanced state in order to move into higher states of flow with the UEF.

In order to fully understand this, one needs to begin this journey somewhere in between the dark and the light frequency spectrum to fully allow the teachings to be absorbed. If one currently leans too far towards darkness or deception, then the natural tendency is to repel this work very quickly as not valid because its essential nature is to shine Light into the Darkness, revealing what is hidden. This can be very difficult for one who prefers to keep it there. If one is too far into exploring only Light spectrums without engaging the darker aspects of Self, she will also feel repelled because she will not understand the necessity to embrace her darkness in order to transform it and become an empowered being of Light. Ultimately becoming a true Spiritual Warrior is where you want to be focused. This will mean that you understand the need for uncovering the deepest aspects of your dark side and using the light aspects of Self to lift you up out of those fear-based illusions into a sovereign being, balanced in all areas of the full spectrum of Life. This is where a more shamanic approach comes into play when engaging these realms – the spiritual worlds. By being willing to shamanically journey into the various scenarios that you keep hidden or private to the outer world, you are able to fully explore the information that is locked up in your ability to maintain the facade. The music provides you with these darker, hidden landscapes for deeper explorations.

Our work is not presented as sugar-coated words without depth; this is pure sonic information that you can assimilate once you fully understand the nature of these teachings. Going beyond your need for linear language as a method of learning and attaining knowledge, we reach out into the Universal Energy Field and connect with the multidimensional realms of Light and Dark in order to unify the full scope of our being. Your DNA is encoded with all these potentials, and while it has been limited in a way to only provide access to what you have needed thus far to live life on Planet Earth, there is so much more within your codex that you can access.

The Sonic Keys are found in Sound. Let us repeat that so you fully understand the importance of this statement. The Sonic Keys that unlock your DNA codes are found in consciously produced Sound. Sound is the magical key you have been waiting for to awaken these higher aspects of Self. Our world is filled with sound; however, it is the unique patterns and sequences that are required to fully access your higher DNA codes. Mystical images, magical phrases crafted by magi who understand this, are all appearing now on the planet to gift those ready with these access codes. We are here to offer this to you in the form of multidimensional sounds that are then translated into musical soundscapes. Our Quantum Sonic Empowerment Technology (QSET) music becomes your magical talisman that can be utilized anytime, anywhere, allowing you to shift situations in your life to a higher vibration whenever you need it. If you are serious about Activating your DNA and have moved beyond the need to quantify strands or follow linear constructs, then we offer you the most powerful sound-based tool on the planet at this time fully focused on the process of DNA Activation.

The Awakening & Activation

Activating your DNA is about awakening dormant potentials and tapping into the multidimensional aspects of the Human Species that have been dormant, waiting for the right codes to unlock the doors. It is fully actualized through the profound embrace of heartfelt feelings and a lifelong commitment to walking the Sacred Path. It is about fully becoming a spiritual being of Light embodying a human form – the ultimate alchemical transformation.

The "activation" of this stored information is a necessary and pivotal initiation to release what you are not while simultaneously integrating the Divine Gnosis of what you truly are – experiential knowledge. This is one of the most important and necessary steps to awaken and tangibly actualize your soul's purpose for your current incarnation. The term "activated" means that your DNA is now ready to move towards the actions and actualizations that are based on the directives you will be intending. Understand that just because you have started the DNA activation process by any of the other available approaches, that it is only the beginning. That was merely Step One into a very vast realm of unlimited possibilities.

There are many techniques and schools of thought on how to activate the DNA – from words, visualizations and affirmations, to formulas and constructs. No matter which approach or technique you choose to follow, including ours, the genuine process requires resolve that eventually becomes impeccable intent in your day-to-day encounters with the world around you. The world around you is the mirror for what is taking place within you, and by keenly observing and monitoring your 3D reality, you are better able to adjust your DNA to maintain continual increases to your Light Quotient. The adventure becomes a vision quest and a live, real-life shamanic journey that opens the path of your True Becoming. It is neither transient, trivial nor a fad. The genuine process, however you arrive there, requires engagement of the Self, building in stages of integration to a profound connection and communion with the multidimensional energy that is Life itself.

The process of activating your multi-strand DNA may require a letting go and shedding of outmoded thoughts and beliefs, relationships and career paths that are no longer in alignment with your true path. In fact anything that does not bring you deeper fulfillment and connection to your unique gifts and your inner Truth will gradually fade away. This path takes time for changes to unfold in alignment with your Higher DNA Blueprint, which requires much patience and perseverance. If you are the impatient type this is probably not the path for you at this time as the results are subtle and build up over time. Layer by layer, the foundations are built to create solid structures reflecting tangible results. Initiations into each successive realm of Light requires a buildup of energy preceding it, and often the trail of situations and circumstances you need to experience in order to break through into that next level of initiation are initially seen as negative and often very difficult. However as you grow and learn to evolve through these situations, you see the higher perspective and necessity of the teachings received. As you continue on the journey, more and more clarity is available to you so that you can move more quickly through these various scenarios. This is where the acceleration process can occur, and you realize you are truly on your journey and that you are always moving forward regardless of the current lessons you may be integrating. We cannot tell you what your evolving Truth is, or what you should ultimately do with it, for IT is unique for everyone. We can promise you that you will come to understand it as you gradually immerse yourself more deeply into the soundscapes.

As your encoded information is released, it will flood the cells with vital energy, raising the vibration of the physical, the energy body and beyond.

We can tell you that whether you choose to engage or not in the process of your becoming, you are connected to all sentient life, dimensions and energy on this Planet. As Mother Earth goes through her initiation, so do you. Your free will choice is to do it consciously or not. Wisdom, the wisdom of not just the mind but of the Soul, the wisdom of heartfelt feeling and full-body knowingness, shares with you that the only way though this time of the Global exposure and integration of the Shadow is to do what you came here to do – DO WHAT YOU CAME HERE TO DO. In order to do that, you must dive deeply into your consciousness (sub, mid and super) past all the layers of fear in order to see clearly.

Anyone who is living in the projections of the imagination alone will learn that they must now embrace the Work of Self-Alchemy until it merges into Joyous Play. Resistance to the process of becoming only feeds the downward spiral. Each that chooses to emerge and unfold like a Shining Lotus from the planetary darkness and stays the course, plugging more Light into the planetary grid by living their visions as a shining example to others, activate not only their DNA (our definition: Divine Numinous Archetypes) but the oversoul DNA connection of the planet itself.

From our enhanced perspective, anyone who is waiting for the aliens to save them or some spiritual master or guru to take their pain away through some gift or state of grace, is buying into an illusion perpetuated to keep you powerless. We as an evolving species on this beautiful planet, no longer have the time for these childhood games. It is time for us to collectively grow up. We say this again and will say it as many times as is necessary – this Global Initiation requires your active participation. Wake Up – Engage. YOU are that which you have been waiting for. When you reach out with sincere intent and take action, give of yourselves through smiles, through the shining emergence of that which is truly You, through action, through support to spiritual resources that nourish you; you begin to merge and co-create with higher principles. You participate in the creation, building the foundations of an open, abundant, free and just society – a wondrous place to grow into and Become, a merging of the inner and outer in which Nature reveals her most sacred secrets and gifts. This is the forging of the Grail of Light, the emergence of Heaven On Earth as we walk in the 5th dimensional realms of being – the 5th World of Light.

What is of more importance than that? In that Light, any procrastination, excuses and wishful thinking fade into insignificance. In what kind of Now do you live, breathe, and have your being? What is the most open potential future that you can envision, and how, through your actions, is the energy of these higher visions flowing and cascading into the zero-point connection that is your Now? How much will you truly allow this energy to change your Life? True mastery always begins with Self – the self of flesh and bone, of blood and sinew, of form and function, of mind and spirit. Honor you Body Temple, for it is your gateway to the Stars.

We give you genuine tools of sound, of Music, the Universal language and communion. We give you a transmission from a genuine, open and sincere source whose lineage spans time, dimensions and planetary and galactic systems. We are required, through Love and Honor, to share further dimensions of You, with You, in a responsible and "real" manner, so that you may integrate the energies and utilize them efficiently in your day-to-day existence. Thus the majesty of what our musical offerings convey may sometimes be cloaked in subtlety. This is part of a grand design to invite you to go deeper, to extract the nectar of what the music really contains – a deeper reflection of the highest and best of You. Active participation is necessary to utilize these Sonic Keys and activate the hidden potentials. When you THINK you have it, you have only just begun. When you truly FEEL it, the genuine adventure is underway. Fully Engage.

> *Certain resonant frequencies have profound effects on the codes within the DNA, keys that have been waiting for thousands, perhaps millions of years for the right evolutionary sequence to be activated.*

The DNA Activation LevelOne series is the foundation – not the ultimate reflection of transcendent experience. We give you that which you require in proper timing. This is where you begin the adventure no matter whether you are a beginner or one who has been on the path for some time. These foundational frequencies must be in place prior to adding the structures, roadways and pathways of the further levels. They contain vast dimensions of experience; however, they simply lay the groundwork for what is to come. All of the other soundscapes in our catalog are also important to extend or emphasize various aspect of the LevelOne foundation. Each will give you the necessary expansions needed in specific areas. As you work through each soundscape, pieces of the puzzle that are You will come together, and you will start to feel this wholeness and unification merging in all areas of your life. You will be guided by your inner compass as to when to move on, trying not to dwell too long in one space. If you find that you are getting stuck or feeling blocked in certain areas, it may be time to ingest new frequencies from a new soundscape or repeat a previous one in order to move through it.

After the integration phase of the DNA Activation LevelOne, move to the DNA 1.5 Lucidity soundscape to really begin the building of the sonic bridges to the DNA.L2 series. DNA 1.5 will further flush out any of the density or darkness that has been lurking and hiding from your awareness. It will assist you in raising your lucidity in both awake and sleeping states, engaging you deeply in the shamanic realms of consciousness. Once you reach a comfort level with this, then it is time to begin the adventure with the six soundscapes that comprise the DNA.L2 series. By this time, your life should be set up in such a way that you are fully walking your path of Light and that you are moving steadily in alignment with your higher potentials. This means you are starting tangible works on your mission parameters; the deeper reason you incarnated at this time. By the time you are ready for this step, it will be clear to you, and you will have walked through many landscapes of both dark and light to get to this place of balance and empowerment. Stepping into the DNA.L2 series is a strongly-stated gesture of respect and understanding of the work, and the Universe will respond in magical ways to this level of commitment within you.

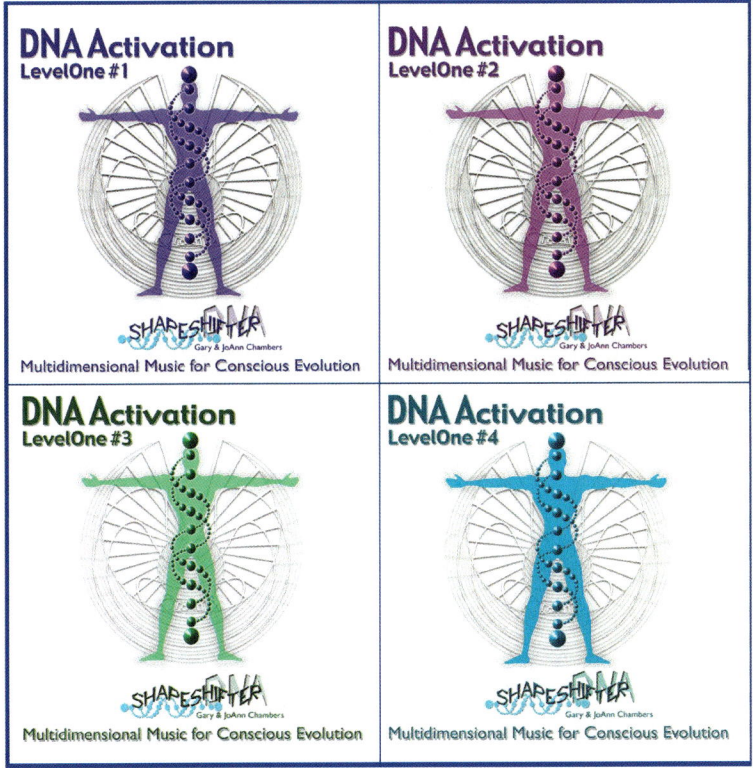

Figure 2. The DNA Activation LevelOne series includes 4 soundscapes.

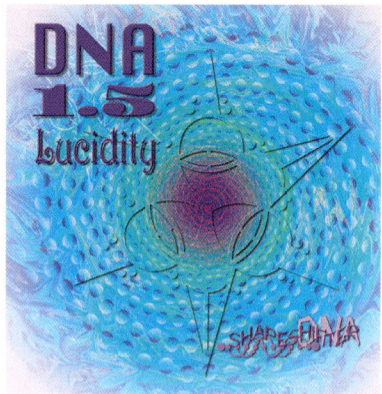

Figure 3. DNA 1.5 Lucidity is a single soundscape.

Figure 4. The DNA.L2 series consists of 6 soundscapes.

Signs of Emergence

Your interest in this topic of exploration and its potentials indicates that you have already started the activation process. The gauge for knowing that your activation is evolving is in the sense of joy, passion and vast love you begin to experience throughout your day to day life. Your life begins to change in positive and tangible ways that cannot be denied when you look back after a few months. A deepened sense of knowingness emerges from somewhere deep within you that you are part of something amazing that is rising up through all of humanity. You will begin to sense a greater spectrum of connection to all things around you. A certain type of flow-like feeling begins to occur in your life. Your intuition starts to emerge along with your psychic/ESP abilities, and synchronicities start to increase and happen daily. Magical possibilities start to become real again as you gain a deeper awareness of the power in your imagination and fantasy worlds to create tangible manifestations in your 3D life. New levels of hope and optimism start to rise up more frequently. Of course this is not going to be your predominant experience until you learn to fully integrate the concepts throughout your life consistently, but even the momentary flashes you start to receive will spark your inner passion to begin creating and manifesting. There will be work to do on your part to adjust your thinking, your beliefs and perceptions about reality and the possibilities that now exist for you.

The validation that you will receive from the energetic sustenance within these soundscapes will be in the positive effects and gifts that you allow yourself to experience and integrate into your life. Your observations and perceptions will begin to shift showing you the synchronistic connections that are beginning to unfold for you. This will be reflected in all areas. You will become more and more aware that there is a subtle magical energy penetrating all your interactions with life. As you become more adept at setting your intent and directing the flows of energy using the music as your magical talisman to guide the flowing nature of reality, you will begin to understand the connections and how they are being made for you.

You will come to understand that multidimensional sound is an important sustenance that feeds your body temple and your body of Light – a sacred food. The sacred use of these Multidimensional-Holographic Frequency Packets (MFPs) have been withheld from you by that aspect of humanity that focuses their primary attention and activity in the lower realms. These realms are filled with deception, manipulation and control on many levels. We leave to you the purpose of this, as there are many variations and themes as to the reasons for this deception. Know this: you too hold resonance to these realms as it is encoded in your

DNA from many previous incarnations. The resonance you still hold with this energy is an aspect of the lack, limitation and fear that you still carry. This is part of the darkness you will be working on releasing with the daily use of the soundscapes. Regardless of this, it is time to reclaim your Power and shine your brightest Light on the planet.

> *The music creates a coherent, multidimensional wave of energy that harmonizes your environment, which you can ingest into your Light Body, your cellular memory and your DNA.*

We are here at this time to share with you these powerful sonic transmissions so that you can use them to recover this potent energy for your illumination and potential transcendence. As you have developed a hunger for food to nourish the physical body, you will begin to develop a hunger for higher octaves of sound that nourishes you energetically, providing much needed sustenance to feed your etheric bodies, your Body of Light.

Certain combinations of resonant frequencies have profound effects on the codes within the DNA, keys that have been waiting for thousands, perhaps millions of years for the right evolutionary sequence to be activated. As a tuning fork generates waves in the air creating a certain pitched sound, current synthesizer technology if utilized with awareness, is able to create a full-range harmonic spectrum that Modulates the Lifewave and activates the codes. Our sincere intent is to assist in raising the vibration of the physical to a more expanded level, reaching the full potential of Spirit manifested in matter. The Sonic Key will fit the lock; the veils will be lifted. As the encoded information is released, it will flood the cells with vital energy, empowering the vibration of the physical, the energy bodies and beyond. You will sense this happening as you begin to listen and to dissolve your awareness into these soundscapes. The more sensitive and aware you are to subtle energy fields, the more you will know this to be true. As you continue letting go into the sounds, you will develop this subtle awareness.

Resonance leads to an implicate higher order. Instead of repairing something that is dis-eased, our approach is to simply invoke this higher blueprint – a more expansive state of spontaneous regeneration. The

LevelOne soundscapes begin to prepare you for the more profound stages of individual and collective evolution yet to be revealed. To integrate the true energy of transformation, you must fully embrace that which you are. The DNA.L2 soundscapes align you with the blueprint of your incarnational directives so that you can carry out the work you came here to accomplish in this lifetime.

Because you each have free will, you always have the choice of how deep you immerse yourself (by this we refer to the "aware personality matrix"), into the vibrational space we have created. We are activating a higher level, more integrated energy field not only within your inner being but also in your outer environment as well – into your living space, your activities, your place of work – wherever these soundscapes are played. Consider the positive implications of freely acting upon this information. Harmony, expansion and an increased quotient of Light will uplift your vibration and therefore through resonance, the vibration of those around you and your interaction with the world will move into higher states of flow. New opportunities will manifest in greater attunement to your heart's desires. Synchronistic events will emerge in your ongoing Vision Quest, and you will initiate a life full of wonder and magic each day, not the kind that knocks you over the head, but a subtle awareness that you are connected to so much more.

You must make the inner decision to lovingly immerse yourself and trust in the process because you wish to move forward, to transcend inertia, to grow, evolve, whatever you term it. Belief is a powerful key, as it is in all things. We create a pool, a reservoir of energy attuned to the common ground of a shared planetary vibration; you use it in a positive manner how you will.

Exploring the Potentials & Possibilities

While every person will have a different experience when using these soundscapes, we have found that there is some common ground. There is an immediate awareness that the sounds are new and unusual to the ear, perhaps the thought will emerge that this is not music as you know music to be. Along with this awareness comes a sense of deep resonance and a feeling of "coming home." If you can understand that these sounds emanate from a vibrational realm that is very deeply connected to The Source of All That Is, then this awareness of coming home will make more sense to you. It is important to move past any preconceived notion of what the music should sound like. Initially some sound patterns may even evoke unpleasant or uncomfortable feelings. The music will reflect aspects of yourself where energy is stuck or blocked, and further work will need to be done by you to move it forward and release the next level of the codes. These are evolutionary sounds, and they are meant to move energy, not just maintain a baseline status quo.

You will come to know your Self better and feel more connected and grounded in your body than you realized possible. The music constantly stimulates the innate resonance you have with your Soul Essence. As you listen more and more deeply, you will have moments of intense feelings of inner peace and acceptance of your life path as it is now. This Soul Level Awareness is something that becomes more expansive as you immerse yourself for longer periods of time in alignment with Source Vibration. You will start to seek answers to the deeper questions about life and existence, like: "Who Am I?", "How did I get here?", "What is my purpose?","What am I capable of becoming?", "What is my higher mission work of service?" As you dive into the soundscapes, answers to these questions and more will start to surface in your aware consciousness.

The same 3D experiences and challenges may present themselves in your reality, but they won't stick and become a part of your being as predominantly as before. The emotional world filled with interactive dramas will begin to subside. You will learn to keep the vibration of your spiritual identity, your Higher Self Matrix, above it all and not be so affected by the density of 3D mundane details. You will no longer carry the weight of emotional baggage around with you all the time, nor will you seek to drain others to support your needs. You will feel a sense of self-empowerment rising up within you all the time as you grow in your awareness and connection to the greater ALL. You will learn to be in this world but not of it; as you discover the gifts of holding higher levels of vibration and expanded states of awareness as you interact with the various scenarios and lessons presented along your journey of becoming Self aware. No longer will the negative situations in your life hold you back , as they will come to be seen as challenges that you move through in order to reclaim your personal power. You will see the higher purpose in these events and move through them more quickly because you will release the victim consciousness & realize you are responsible for the reality you experience. You will clearly be more aware of when your Lower Self matrix is taking charge. As you take full responsibility now for all situations and events, you know that you made direct and indirect decisions in each that have led you to where you are in the moment. This knowingness allows for greater levels of self-empowerment knowing that you are fully responsible for what you are experiencing at all times.

> *The DNA Activation soundscapes were created with the INTENT to unlock and activate the codex within the DNA through frequency, sound and vibration.*

You will rest deeper so that your body gets the sound sleep necessary to grow your Light and expand, thereby initiating profound states of self healing. Learning how to initiate deeper shamanic states between your awake and asleep states, you will be able to direct the energy as needed for the healing of Self on all levels. Dreams will be become a nocturnal storyline to guide your choices and decision making during the day. Symbolic messages from Spirit will be gifting you with many levels of information and guidance as you become more aware and expanded in your understanding of communications with the Universal Energy Field. Synchronicity becomes an everyday occurrence in your life. You will be more pro-active and less re-active to life's day-to-day challenges. You will learn how to be more in a state of flow with the various events you engage with. This allows you more time to make decisions and choices that are supportive of your higher path than those that will redirect you back into the inertial downward spirals of dark and dense scenarios. A true sense of calm will come over you, and you will be more trusting of the big picture and less bothered by life's details. Joy will be more matter of fact in your everyday world. Your appearance and facial expression will soften, and you will feel at the beginning of something exciting and brand new, continuously. Doldrums, boredom and same-old same-old will be expressions unknown to your vocabulary. Gratitude and Love will be expressions that you feel at the core of your everyday self.

We are proposing that you consider a new way of viewing your reality as a multidimensional consciousness within the realm of 3D matter and redirect your intent so that DNA Activation becomes a main theme of your spiritual growth work. This orientation will bring all aspects of your explorations into a seamless tapestry that becomes the full potential of what you are. When combined with any other teachings that you have strong resonance with, deeper connections can be made to enhance your understanding of the more intricate levels within them. The music itself is a Sonic Mystery School of vast proportions, but you are the one who directs the flows of information based on your areas of interest. When you initiate conscious communication with your DNA, the core level organizational matrix of your being, multiple dimensions of depth and meaning will unfold in everything that you experience.

Another very common experience each time you listen is that you become aware of new sounds and patterns. You will find even after years of listening, this will continue to be so. The soundscapes are composed multidimensionally so that they actually release new frequencies/sounds as you evolve and increase your Light Quotient. This is because your personal vibrational pattern is changing and shifting as you evolve, so the things that you focus on will be different and the multidimensional mirror of vibrational content contained within the music will reveal new facets for your enlightenment and exploration. Your clairaudient abilities are literally increasing. It responds to you the more you interact with it. Think of them as an organic tangible form that you engage with as you would any teacher or therapist.

The more you reach out to IT, the more IT reaches back to You.

Engaged & Focused Listening

We recommend that with each new soundscape that you listen to it at least 7 times in a deep state of meditation before moving on to the next soundscape. Background or casual listening does not count towards the 7, so take your time and don't feel you need to rush the process. You will still continue listening to all the previous soundscapes too once you integrate each new one. This initial listening process is important so that you develop a deeper relationship with each soundscape before moving to another one. The four soundscapes in the LevelOne series lays the foundation upon which to grow spiritually, accrete more light, raise your vibration and ground your energy.

As you shift your overall frequency and expand through new ways of interacting and being in your 3D reality, you will continue to experience the soundscapes in new and deepening ways. Not because they have changed but because you have. As you take on more Light, you can literally hear sounds that are happening in other dimensional levels, which enables you to hear new sounds that you didn't hear before. This reflects an increase in your ESP abilities, specifically your clairaudient ability as mentioned, but it also affects clairvoyance and clairsentience too. We have been listening to LevelOne since 1989, and we are continually awed and humbled by the profound shifts, new paradigms, more expanded perception and levels of being they deliver.

Use the highest quality player that you have, as the better the sound system, the more expansive the sounds you hear will be. You want to have a good mid-range tweeter and a sub-woofer to really get the full range of sounds available in the soundscapes; home theaters are great. You want the sounds to reflect from the acoustic space of the entire room, surrounding you in a powerful vibrational matrix, so during your sessions you will want to turn the volume up.

The music is channeled from a place of pure intent and can be a multi-dimensional resource of evolutionary knowledge and wisdom.

In addition to hearing the music, it is very important to FEEL as deeply as you are able; let your physical body, down to the cellular level and up through the auric layers and beyond, blend with the sounds and joyfully dance to the resonant frequencies. Let go, allowing your consciousness to travel on these waves of sound and energy patterns – learn how to become energetically aware and less physically focused. Let yourself be guided by your own inner knowingness, while also being mindful of where you are traveling. Ultimately you want to shift into Becoming the Music, ultimately dissolving all sense of the physical form, moving into spontaneous out-of-body states and learning how to shamanically journey through many dimensional realms. Our Activate your DNA DVD Training Program will help you to learn various techniques which you can then expand upon to build your skills from there. Take a look at these images in Figure 5. to get a visual interpretation on what it is you are working towards achieving. While it may seem easy to do, it takes years of practice to continually perfect this technique. Letting go is not really something we do easily, but it can be learned by using this technique.

Figure 5. Shows the various stages one goes through as they learn how to listen more deeply to multidimensional music. Gradually one learns to Become the Music and ultimately dissolving into the sounds, losing sense of the physical world but still maintaining an aware level of consciousness.

Headphones are great too, as many of the headphones on the market today provide a very expansive range of high quality sound. Headphones provide movement of the sound fields within your headspace which adds a different dimension to the experience. Be sure that you have a good set, as otherwise you will lose a lot of the sound quality. Try to mix it up as much as you can by listening on different sound systems, but when you are really going to do some deeper work, use the best sound delivery system you have available.

We don't recommend compressing the sound files via any type of MP3 compression format, as this will remove some of the high and low frequencies. If you want to transfer to an Ipod or similar, use a .wav or .aif file – also FLAC or Apple Lossless are equivalent quality to the CD and reduces the file size quite a bit. However if you are just using it for light background music, then it is ok to use the MP3 for that purpose.

It is important to make your listening space as positive and uplifting as possible. You may feel the need to smudge, to utilize aromatherapy or other personal sacred rituals to cleanse your environment. Invoke a feeling of love, safety, sanctuary and protection with deep feeling and sincerity. Connect to whatever aspect of Source Vibration/All That Is that you relate to, with whatever methods feel right for you. The more you put into the process, the more will be returned to you.

This is not just music you listen to only with your ears. This is a full body experience that ultimately engages all your bodies in the process – physical, emotional, mental and spiritual. When you work deeply with them, you should be in a contemplative, relaxed place such as meditation or a shamanic state. In addition to listening with conscious awareness throughout the journey, you may also choose to let the music play in the background in the environments where you live, work, play and drive. As you become more aware of the subtleties of the matrix of Light within the Universal Energy Field (UEF), you will be able to sense how the sounds create vibrational patterns in your living spaces. We suggest you play them during any activity in which it will not be distracting. This can be working, playing sports, creating projects, reading, studying, doing yoga and also healing, massage or spa type sessions.

Using them before, during and after sleep is the most profound way to work with them without interrupting any of your activities or your current life's schedule. The soundscapes will enhance the rest you get as well as deepening the dreaming experience, a vital aspect of developing an expanded consciousness. If you think about sleep as being a time when the egoic mind drops its guard so to speak, the thinking process that is always active, going over the details of your everyday world, it only makes sense that this is also "primetime" to communicate with and receive guidance from other dimensions. The soundscapes will heighten your dream travel capacities, awaken lucid dreaming abilities and enable you to begin directing where you want to go to receive the guidance you are ready for via shamanic journeying. If you consider for a moment the awake state versus the sleep state, your goal is to attain conscious awareness in between these two where you are able to hold focus, set intent and work on manifesting your desires. This is a significantly different place from the constant chattering of the mind. This is where the truest form of manifestation generation is found. The mind is not quiet, but it is sharply focused. This is what we call the shamanic state of awareness; a place where you control the position of your assemblage point.. It is a spiritually advanced skill to be able to hold this state of awareness for longer and longer periods of time. This is a place of extreme power and potential. This is beyond basic meditation and moves into the deeper levels of manifesting and directing energy flows. This is an evolutionary human ability we all have but have lost our connection to through all the noise and disharmonious sounds we are immersed in each day. This is one very powerful aspect of DNA Activation that will awaken in you.

As for falling asleep while listening to the music during meditation, you will go through many stages of learning to engage with the frequencies while trying to remain aware. The ultimate goal is to be engaged while fully conscious in a meditative state. You will move into a deep theta/delta brain wave state developing an energetic relationship with them – a place where a form of dialog with or without words can occur. Gradually losing your aware consciousness can extend the meditative state into the sleep state, while deepening your levels of exploration and travel without the ego mind. Be aware, however, that the ego can induce sleep to escape the "work" of spirit when it knows accountability to the path of Light is being called for. Consciously sleeping with them as opposed to escaping is a powerful shamanic technique. We suggest you play them at a lower volume throughout the night while dropping deeper into expanding your clairaudient ability to hear more and more layers of sounds, while still feeling the vibrations in the subtlest layers of your auric field.

One might conclude that human languages are a reflection of the patterns within the DNA codex.

DNA Strands as Metaphors

First, let us say that there is no end to your expansion and evolving. If there were an end point to achieve in this reality, what would be the point? Your evolution is an ongoing process as long as you are in the physical vehicle, and then beyond that there is much more for you to discover. But since you are here now in this Earth based reality, we suggest you consider focusing primarily on what it is you can accomplish here first, while still developing the more expansive abilities for your next evolutionary cycle. The only limitations are the ones you place upon yourself.

We see the number of strands more like a metaphor. Be it 2 or 12 strands, 22, 3000, 144,000 infinitum, the strands represent the infinite potential we have to evolve. Depending on your need to make things complex in your attempt to understand a subject, you can certainly make this one very intricate and involved. Eventually it will all boil down to faith and trust in the inner guidance you are receiving. Ultimately these are all models that will serve to help you in transcending what is believed to be truth by the current belief systems in which you formulate your personal picture of reality and the potential therein. These are transcendent concepts, abstract in nature, and can only be grasped by a mind that is capable of stepping beyond what is known. Walk bravely into the unknown. This is the place where true evolution and innovation occur.

The music creates a coherent multidimensional wave of energy that harmonizes your environment, which you can ingest into your Light Body, your cellular memory and your DNA.

These soundscapes oscillate through the spectrum of manifestation from the two strands through the etheric harmonic overlays that some have semantically termed "the other strands." Consider for a moment what you would imagine a fully functional 12-strand being of Light to be and then ask yourself if it is really possible for you to become that in a short period of time. It wouldn't be advisable even if you could as you would burn out and not be able to integrate the high degree of Light that this would generate.

Rather than get into a contest of who has the most strands activated, enjoy the journey and allow it to unfold like a thousand-petaled lotus. These soundscapes allow you to take the process at the pace that is most comfortable for you to integrate the changes into the worldviews you are currently a part of – be it work, family or social activities. Initially, you may have a lot of house cleaning work to do with yourself, so it may start a little slow. This really all depends on the amount of personal growth work you have done previously. From there, ideally, you will find that you are consistently moving towards higher states of integration in all aspects of your life. This can be an accelerated path, but you are the one who chooses just how fast to set the pace.

> *These soundscapes oscillate through the spectrum of manifestation, from the two strands through the etheric harmonic overlays that some have semantically termed the other strands.*

The Unfolding Process

Some people have an amazing experience right away, while for others it can take some time. If you were to take the first 30 days to work with each CD for a full week and really learn how to drop down into the soundscapes, you will know that something new and wonderful has begun. From there, seeing significant changes in your life and the world around you will begin to manifest within 3 to 6 months of consistent daily listening. From there, the process continues throughout your lifetime as you consciously choose to deepen your experiences and interactions with the Universal Energy Field (UEF).

The frequencies within the soundscapes meet you where you are in your core level intent. If increasing your intelligence is important to your journey and fulfilling your evolutionary path, then yes, the soundscapes will illuminate that capacity of your being and more. You decide where the area of focus is at all times. The first step of the process may just be for you to learn to enjoy the music and see where that leads you. They will ultimately become one of your most powerful teachers and strongest allies in your unfolding path, but as in any relationship, this can take time to develop. You will develop your own patterns of listening and working with them, so just let it all unfold magically without putting too many expectations into the process.

There are many testimonials on our website that you can read from others who have worked with these soundscapes to see what they have experienced, but don't let that set you up to try to achieve what others have. While all the information is a truth and reality for each of the individuals in their personal journeys, it is important to surrender expectation and the tendency to gauge your experience by someone else's reality. Expectation is a ploy of the ego that can serve to cloak and even block the shifts that are ready to occur in your own experience. Remain open and allow for surprise to be your daily experience.

Setting goals is a good idea, as well as recapitulating negative events throughout your life to recapture lost energy which can prevent you from meeting these goals. Rewriting past events from a new perspective will help you to take on more of the Light available in these soundscapes, increasing levels of self-empowerment. When you have done the preparation of inviting higher guidance from Source Vibration into the world you now inhabit, there is nothing more for you to do than to get out of the way of what will be revealed to you. You are endeavoring to create a bridge that will enable you to be in this world but not of it – to "lighten up" the density of matter and form. Your bridge will be unique to you.

You could begin this new adventure by creating a sacred space in your environment with a ceremony surrounding it. This assists you by having a special location where you know that you are there specifically to shift from your 3D self to your more expanded, ethereal self – the aspect of you that exists in the 5th World of Light. This is a place where you will surrender your ego and offer up your heart each day to the vastness from which we came. Once this ceremony becomes a part of your daily pattern, the Universe will resonate with the sincerity of your intent and will respond in kind with a clear and identifiable stream of communication that will deepen with your capacity to hold frequency.

Evolution, by its very nature, is not always what you expect.

It cannot be overstated that we are energetic spiritual beings, temporarily experiencing the density of this dimension by inhabiting a human body. The amount of time from our imagining to our manifesting, from our seeking to our evolving, and from our needing to ask questions versus being the answer to our questions is dependent upon our ability to consistently hold a higher vibrational state. The affirmation of your DNA activation also lies in your capacity to shift your assemblage point and the density of your vibration with less effort and more continuity of flow. When you are activated, you will simply know, and the tendency to question will be of lessening importance. This is an ongoing process with no end point, because evolution never ceases; there is always more.

Complementary Spiritual Work

Any DNA Activation or spiritual development work you are doing or have done so far on your journey will be enhanced by listening to these sonic frequencies. As stated before, DNA activation using these soundscapes is not a one-time experience but an ongoing process that will continue to evolve as you raise your vibration and expand your fields of awareness. They can be used throughout your entire lifetime to support your evolutionary journey. The soundscapes will act as support throughout your ongoing process of becoming which will take many years of dedication and focus. It is advisable to decide from the beginning you are here to enjoy the journey and there is no race to any type of finish line; there is no competition. In fact, if you try to push too hard, you'll end up regressing for a while until you learn how to integrate the new Light you have taken on. Pushing energy will be met with the same in return which can often lead to difficulty, problems and serious life lessons. Learn to move into flow states more and more, releasing the pressure generated from pushing or forcing situations.

If you have received an activation from a healer or a workshop, we consider this just the beginning step. It is like a light switch was turned on in an ancient library full of books. Now your task is to clean up the cobwebs and start looking through those books to see just what information applies to your individual path. This is where the DNA soundscapes will continue to support this unfolding process as it will help you to open books that were not even in your realm of awareness before. The unseen becomes seen; the unknown becomes known and so it goes.

Convergence of Science & Spirituality

Our work emanates from a shamanic approach, one in which connecting directly to Source/God/ALL supersedes the need to provide scientific data. We are approaching this work from a consciousness perspective as opposed to slicing and dicing the DNA. We believe that within our own DNA are the necessary sequences we need to evolve to the next levels of our human abilities. With that said, we do embrace the theories from some of today's leading edge scientifics. We consider ourselves spiritual scientists; willing to explore theories and concepts on the leading edge of consciousness research. We live our lives out on the edge of this wave and bring back information for others to use after we have found substantial results from our personal explorations.

Some science to ponder.... DNA is composed of a hyper-sophisticated language. In the wondrous Body Temple, the "double serpent" DNA strands within the nucleus of each cell, if stretched from end to end, would be over 125 billion miles long. This biotechnology contains over a hundred trillion times as much information as our most sophisticated storage devices. Yet it has been scientifically proven that we use only 3% of the total genetic information available to us; the function of the remaining 97%, representing untapped potential, is yet unknown to conventional science. Much research is currently going on in this field, and they are starting to discover more about this 97% each day. We believe that some of the repeat sequences of this 97% contain information to evolve the energetic structure of the Body Temple, Spirit in form. It is our sincere intent to activate this dormant information through the higher vibrational energy of our Quantum Sonic Empowerment Technology (QSET), creating Multidimensional-Holographic Frequency Packets (MFPs) of potentiated sounds to "Modulate the Lifewave." Going beyond the 2-strand DNA model that our planet's scientists are working with, we explore the concepts/theories that there are additional strands that humans are capable of accessing in addition to the 2. While there is no solid scientific basis in this yet, there are many of the leading-edge scientifics, particularly in the quantum physics field, starting to become more aware of this potential.

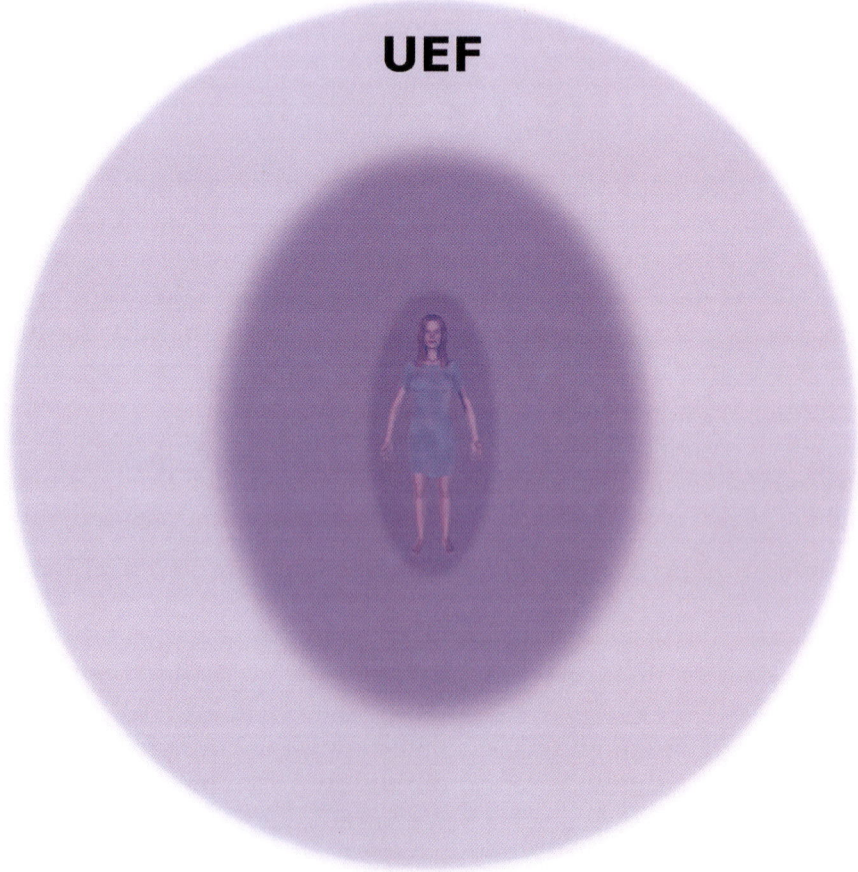

Figure 6. The outer ring represents the Universal Energy Field encompassing the full frequency spectrum of unlimited potentials. The central image of a human is surrounded by the average range of frequencies while the middle ring shows the expansion of one's spectrum of awareness as you start to engage with the DNA Activation Music.

Then consider this from the metaphysical perspective. Our human form, that which exists in the 3D realms of known space that we collectively call reality, is only a small portion of who we are. A larger, more powerful aspect of our being in human form is that we also exist simultaneously in a multidimensional Universe of Light. Our scientific community is steadily moving towards confirming that which the evolving consciousness has acknowledged for millennia, that we are made up of varying degrees of frequencies and that everything is in continuous motion all of the time. Matter only seems solid from the location of the frequency spectrum from which we are viewing it. But when seen with microscopic vision, there is a constant dance of energy. If you explore this from the Powers of 10 or the theory of "As Above, So Below" we begin to see that whether we go inward to the cellular/DNA level or out into deep space that we experience the same quality of energy – both visually and sensory. Through graduated states of harmonic resonance, each successive layer/level/dimension is connected to the others. Your DNA is a receiver, a transmitter and the Grail that holds the Living Light and information of all the myriad dimensions that you are and are connected to. By the direction of your intention, you are ultimately connected to all these realms at all times, and it is your conscious choice as to where you choose to focus your attention.

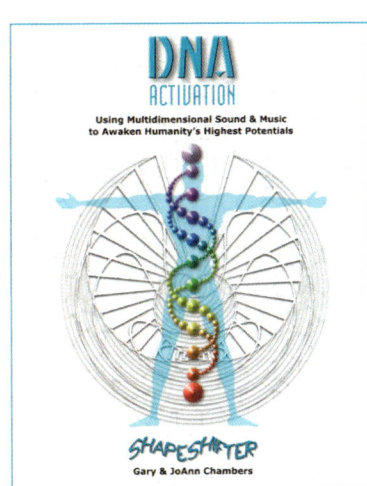

In our book, DNA Activation: Using Multidimensional Sound & Music to Awaken Humanity's Highest Potentials, that accompanies the LevelOne soundscapes, we give a wider range of scientific theories from which you can make some leaps in your consciousness to ultimately find a comfortable place where you can explore further.

We also encourage you to read more about our DNA from many of the various authors and researchers as this knowledge helps build the collective awareness that will ultimately help humanity move past the limitations in our current cultural paradigm. Some of these newer thought-forms include that we are capable of youthing, rejuvenating, self-healing, regenerating, consciously ascending and much more.

Whether you approach this work from a scientific or metaphysical perspective, you can see how you can arrive at a greater understanding of the potentials that await your sincere intention to activate your DNA by becoming fully conscious of the process and actively participating in it on a daily basis.

Multidimensional Sound is the Sonic Key

Sound is the fabric of our entire existence; it is the glue that keeps everything together. Each of us reflects our own personal symphony of sounds. Each individual's life could be scored like a movie soundtrack, featuring every emotion in the spectrum. Many are stuck in a groove playing the same old song with slight variations, over and over again throughout the entire course of their life. As one ages, this spectrum narrows into fixated and frozen patterns of mundane sameness.

These soundscapes invite you to play a new song by learning how to consciously become sound in motion. Through establishing graduated states of harmonic resonance with the sounds in the various soundscapes offered, you expand your spectrum of experiential understanding of the multidimensional realms of Light that we all have access to. The music introduces you to these vistas of potential experiences so that you can choose consciously how to direct the flows of your life path.

Music, sound, modulation, harmonics and vibration are fundamental elements emanating "beyond" and through the core level subatomic of 3D reality. We are energy beings composed of various frequency packets that mesh together to form the matter that we call the human body. A much larger part of who we are exists in the non-visible, etheric realm of energy.

What we know to exist in the realm of 3D reality also exists in higher octaves of Light in varying degrees. These inter-penetrating layers from the physical to the etheric and beyond reach out into the Universal Oneness and connect us to All That Is. These DNA soundscapes were created with the intent to connect these realms into one multidimensional experience in order to create a smooth, seamless transition point from one to the other – to build a unified field composed of frequency maps within this vast, multidimensional territory we call consciousness. Through the process of harmonic resonance between the music and the cells of your bio-energetic matrix, this unified field of Light is established. Once there is resonance, the key factor in the equation becomes your sincere intent to utilize this energetic resource to initiate Unity Consciousness with the Greater ALL, thereby moving you towards the process of choosing to consciously evolve at a more accelerated pace; this is actualized Conscious Evolution. You are now tapping into the collective resource of knowledge and information as well as the Universal realms of Higher Wisdom.

Figure 7. Images shows how the Universal Energy Field runs throughout all known realities unifying everything in a higher state of Oneness, through graduated step of harmonic resonance.

As we evolve as a species, we gradually increase our Light Quotient to be able to exist within the more rarefied dimensional realms of potential realities. This is the evolutionary process in motion. We currently have our 2-strand DNA manifesting in a 3D-level reality; the additional 10+ strand dimensional states that we are working towards activating exist as inter-penetrating overlays in the more subtle realms of vibration and frequency – what is called the etheric world of Spirit. We see this as a holographic network of interconnecting nodes that act as portals and gateways into alternate realities or parallel realities.

Beginning with the LevelOne series, we are activating first-level evolutionary codes within the 2-strand DNA, which creates the base resonance for the additional 10 strands and beyond to become active once the stable foundation has been attained. This is the place to start. The process of activating the DNA is one that requires patience, perseverance and a commitment to maintain focus and balance in 3D reality, while simultaneously expanding your consciousness further out to hold higher and higher frequencies of Light. The soundscapes provide the energetic waves for you to surf with your consciousness which will take you gradually through this evolutionary progression.

Your DNA accumulates all data and sorts and catalogs it constantly. It is your personal connection to what has been termed the Akashic Records, containing information from all of your incarnations, on-world and off-world. It contains links and data to the Matrix of information and conscious experience shared by all sentient life throughout the harmonic Universes – past, present and probable futures.

Through sounds/modulations/harmonics, we initiate a contact first with the 2-strand DNA that exists in 3D. From this point, by establishing a progressive pattern of sympathetic resonance, we begin the process of activating what has been termed the 3rd, 4th, 5th, 6th, 7th, 8th, 9th, 10th, 11th and 12th strands of our DNA – we build a frequency map of these dimensional qualities or states. It is like waking up and re-energizing a part of yourself that has always existed but has been asleep for a very long time. Our soundscapes oscillate through the spectrum of manifestation, from the two strands through the etheric harmonic overlays encompassing the entire 12-dimensional matrix and then beyond that as you are able to engage. We see the 12-strand and 12-dimensional model as an initial place to begin, but we experience many strands and dimensions beyond this awaiting our ability to reach out and connect.

For now, we are concerned with the practical matters and results of a more expansive 2-strand enlightenment in your current life expressions in 3D. Once you become infused with this new energy, you begin to act, think and talk differently. You take on new meanings for your life – that you really can rejuvenate, experience vibrant health and accomplish any of the dreams that you desire. The manifestation process of learning how to be in harmonious co-creation with the energy dynamic that is the world of matter becomes so much more clear to you. Now the actualization of these insights will ground into form, bit by precious bit, as you are willing to let go of that which no longer serves you and act in the honoring of these new awarenesses. The path of higher evolution is to ask to be shown the more expansive aspects of your being and your connection to the collective consciousness of the planet and Source Vibration. As your vibratory field expands and stabilizes, you will synchronistically attract what you need to do your chosen work. The limitation of time and space will no longer hold the same meaning for you as barriers begin to dissolve, which allows you to expand your realm of possibilities tenfold. Understand that all the processes and spiritual growth work you have done thus far, all of them support your DNA Activation process. What you need now is simply to become much more deeply aware of these currents of energy.

The DNA Activation LevelOne soundscapes are an empowering tool and a first level initiation into a vast realm of new possibilities that can begin to manifest – if you so choose. They will assist you to begin to put all the pieces of your personal puzzle together, seamlessly. This allows you to see a more expansive overview of the cloaked areas now coming to Light, of the true multidimensional nature, and flowing wonder and Art of the Game itself.

DNA 1.5 Lucidity will take you to the next steps on this journey by creating the necessary bridge to the architectural realms of the 5th World of Light. Holding lucid awareness during this transitionary phase is a necessary step as it gets more difficult to hold focus and awareness in the higher realms of Light. Following this phase, you should be pretty clear on your work on the planet and at least have some of the templates in place for your creation phase. Then the DNA. L2 soundscapes will begin to accelerate your work on the Planet as you are now aligned with your true path & purpose. Once in harmony with this information, you can then begin the actualization phases of your highest mission parameters.

Harmonic Resonance in Action

Initially the music will establish a resonance with whatever symphony you are currently playing within your Bio-Energetic Matrix.

In a sense, the energetic presence within the sounds will begin to dance with you. The sounds used in these recordings are evolutionary – they are new to the human physiology. As you listen to them, they gently begin to stimulate new neural pathways and synapses throughout your body. This gradually starts to create new perceptions of reality as perceived through your 5 main senses – hearing, sight, smell, touch and taste. In addition, these evolutionary sounds start to awaken your sixth sense, that of intuition and psychic perception. This is the area where much of your dormant potential is hidden, waiting for the right sonic keys to open these doors. The music also opens your heart center to allow more Love and Light energy into your field of awareness which further connects you to the Universal Energy Field (UEF).

In shamanic terms, the music is shifting and altering the direction and flow of your assemblage point – the area within your personal bio-energetic field where you maintain focus. By redirecting this point of focus instead of becoming fixated into grooved patterns of sameness, you begin to widen your frequency spectrum to take in more and more information.

Everything that exists in all dimensions is a combination of frequencies. Various frequencies combined creates vibration, which is sound. So you could say that everything in 3D and beyond has its own unique tonal expression. The music creates a coherent, multidimensional wave of energy that harmonizes with your environment. You can ingest this energy into your body of Light (etheric template) activating your cellular memory and your DNA. This in turn stimulates activity in the physical body, and the neural system initiates movement throughout the energy body and chakra system which ultimately extends into the holographic field around you. You become a walking, talking field of potentiated energy in motion seeking connections with similar and matching vibrational signatures. You are a vortex of Light-encoded potentials waiting to align and connect with other like vibrations.

Your chakras are doorways into multiple worlds and dimensions.

The sounds in the DNA music encompass infinite combinations and patterns that are available to anyone who wants to explore altered states of consciousness – a smörgåsbord of potentials, one would say. They contain millions of possibilities available in the full spectrum of the human DNA. We call them Multidimensional-Holographic Frequency Packets (MFPs) to describe these combinations of empowering possibilities. When you learn how to become sound and drop into the flow of these musical soundscapes, you establish a resonance with all these MFPs by connecting with the Universal Energy Field (UEF). From there, it is up to you to guide the ship in the direction that you want to go. This is not something that happens to you, it is something you direct with your INTENT. This is the Sonic Key that opens doors to your higher potentials.

Through sympathetic resonance, which states that when something that is formerly passive or neutral in nature is introduced to external vibrations to which it has some harmonic likeness, it responds with movement of some kind. 97% of what the scientific community has designated "junk DNA," in truth, holds the infinite reach of our hidden potential. Understand that the 3% you are using now is what you need to maintain the physical form along with the codes that keep the Soul connected until death. The untapped 97% is lying dormant and/or asleep, and ready to awaken when you give the green light. This aspect of mankind has been dormant until a time when our consciousness developed to such a place that we would seek to find the hidden sonic keys to unlock the doorways to our higher gifts – a time when it would become necessary for our very survival to evolve and assume a higher role in the Universal realms of Light.

There is safety and comfort in the known, but there are varying degrees of complacency and inertia that settle in when your spirit and passions are not being nurtured, engaged or challenged to be more. For many this was cut off when you were just a child by your parents who themselves were unable to actualize their higher visions. The vibrations and frequencies in all of our soundscapes are attuned to assist you in moving past the constant chatter of the ego mind: the doubts, resistances, illusions of fear and limitation that keep us from being fully conscious and reaching for more. A small inkling of that more is the awareness that your DNA is a receiver, a transmitter and the Grail that holds the Living Light and information of all the myriad dimensions that you are and are connected to. The key to unlocking this potential is found in graduated degrees of resonant frequencies – the Sonic Keys. As the stored encoded information is released, it will flood the cells with vital energy, raising the vibration of the physical, the energy body and beyond. These soundscapes are part of the new sustenance required for the physical, emotional, mental and spiritual bodies to evolve into the next levels of human existence. When you start to perceive and accept with radical, full-body awareness that you are composed of vibrational fields of energy, you will come to understand that sound and frequency become part of the food that feeds and sustains this energy vessel.

Spiritual Evolution

It is common at first to take a class or a workshop and read books in the areas in which one feels the most resonance to the work that they came here to do. With each new technique or area of study you learn, you then integrate and incorporate that into the tapestry that is becoming YOU. Each piece may fill you with new wisdom or knowledge, but there may be gaps in your life experience that may make full integration more challenging and time-consuming. We speak of the full integration of body, emotion, mind and spirit – all must be in unity and harmony with each other and move forward with balance if you want to progress steadily. The soundscapes unveil more of the resonant field of potential that is You. Using sound/frequency as a bridge, they connect the neural pathways necessary so that you can assimilate these teachings on a higher level much more quickly. They do not impose any fixed dogma on you. They connect the dots for you so that you can complete the puzzle yourself. The soundscapes are like a Tabula Rasa, a blank slate, which you fill up with whatever is unique to your special purpose and mission during this incarnation.

The planetary shift is accelerating and will continue to do so with or without your active participation. These soundscapes are an initiatory process to shift the receptive listener's vibration into a resonant alignment with the frequencies now occurring as we move into the next dimensional spiral. We are simply giving you tools that you may choose to utilize to raise your vibrational level to be in alignment with the evolutionary current, rather than being burned out or swept away by it or feeling continually out of sync with the world around you. They will assist you to gradually and steadily sync yourself up with the 2012 to 2032 alignment codes, enabling you to move through these timelines with more flow, ease and abundance in all areas of your life. As the 5th World/Heaven on Earth templates are being laid down within the greater matrix of all life, you will notice day by day that you are always in alignment with these influxes of higher energy. The DNA Activation LevelOne series are building the multidimensional frequency maps to allow you to begin to gracefully explore these new realms filled with creative potential, thereby creating a smoother transition process from each dimensional state to the next.

Even though many of you have been engaged in personal/spiritual growth for years and even lifetimes, there are still experiential gaps within each of us that need to be harmonized in order to fully attain balance. A high degree of body, mind, emotion, and spiritual balance is necessary to begin the journey required for the conscious ascension process. Any area of weakness will be called to change. These soundscapes will illuminate these imbalanced frequency bands for you so that you can work on the appropriate areas of your life in order to come to a balanced state of consciousness. This may include dietary changes, release work, emotional clearing, exercise, pastlife clearing, karmic release work, soul retrieval, more meditation or discipline in your spiritual practices, etc. – it will be different for each.

They will enhance any process that you are currently working on and provide you with a range of frequencies that will enable you to receive your own guidance on the directions you need to take in order to actualize your full potential. This music is channeled from a place of clear intent and can be a multidimensional resource of evolutionary knowledge and wisdom. Over time, one can learn how to tap into certain frequency bands and bring that information back into the 3D level of reality that is formed of language. The listener is invited to resonate with and surf the waves of sound to assimilate vistas of experience beyond the limitations of logical thought. Learning how to translate this sonic information is a process of stepping down the transmission and translating it into language/words/thoughts which leads to tangible actions and ultimately a greatly enhanced manifestation process, which contains the abundance you are seeking. Once you really get this concept, so much of your current dysfunctional-like reality can dissolve, and you can start living your life from a higher perspective on a daily basis.

All languages emerged from transmissions from the DNA itself to further direct wo/mankind's evolution at certain points on the timestream.

Part of consciously connecting your DNA to the greater field of Light means that you are going to tap into an unlimited resource of Universal Intelligence. Certain aspects of learning can be done through osmosis because the Universal Energy Field (UEF) contains ALL that has been and will be. This correlates to what some have called the akashic records, which contains personal as well as Universal information. This process, in turn, activates dormant knowledge and potentials within you, and you become capable of increased intelligence and advanced wisdom. As the unique sound patterns open up new neural pathways beyond your current limits, you tap into this vast reservoir. All languages emerged from transmissions from the DNA itself to further direct wo/mankind's evolution at certain points on the timestream. This means you can tap into these same currents of information streams. One might conclude that human languages are a reflection of the patterns within the DNA codex.

We suggest that if you are in the process of studying anything, that you play the music in the background while you study. Set up the intent that as you are studying, the higher part of you is absorbing the data for recall at a later time as needed. You can also program yourself prior to going to sleep with suggestions that the information will become a part of your field and that you will remember it as needed. Many areas of your life with benefit from attaining this type of knowledge.

A Lifetime of Empowerment

The great thing about these soundscapes is that they continually shift and change as you evolve. So that means you can listen to them for many years, even your entire lifetime, and still feel you are receiving more levels of empowerment from them. Your experiences with them will deepen over the years and at times, they will seem to release a whole new level of information as a result of the various work you are doing in your life and on your path. When you are ready to move on to DNA 1.5 and then the DNA.L2 program, you will just get an inner prompting letting you know it is time. Even then, you can still always return back to the LevelOne series and engage with them.

Initially, we suggest you take you time with each CD going through them one at a time to fully integrate each soundscape. The idea is to feel that the sounds have harmonized within your entire bio-energetic field and that your outer life also reflects this. It may bring up areas that need further work from you in many areas of your life. You may need to do some extensive detoxing and cleansing of the physical body to be able to take on the higher levels of Light energy. This will also require shifts in your diet and the release of any addictive patterns you may currently be engaged with. Your life may have toxic relationships that need to shift to a higher state of Love and Compassion. Your career path may be moving in a direction that is not in alignment with your higher path and purpose which may require you to change jobs or careers or redefine what you are doing in a different way. You may also find that the location you are living in is not suitable to your new life path. Once you agree to engage with the journey to really become all that you can become, your higher self will assist you in making all the necessary adjustments needed to align your life with that intent. As they say, be careful what you ask for.

This is a spiritual journey and does require dedication, perseverance and commitment to walk the path with integrity and impeccability. When you step up into that place, you need to be prepared to review the life you have created thus far and take full responsibility for all those manifestations. Whether they are positive or negative situations, they were all necessary for your evolutionary growth at the time. You will come to know that divine order has been overseeing all aspects of your life with great Love through each of your lessons. It is important to continually work with some recapitulation (life review) techniques as this will help you to continually move the energy as it emerges as opposed to having it get stuck or lodged in an old groove that is often difficult to move out of. We usually recommend that one utilizes the appropriate counseling and guidance sessions along with this work.

We offer various types of spiritual guidance services along with our music to help you to understand the various steps and stages that you go through on this journey. JoAnn is skilled at reading the energetic state of the full bio-energetic body of Light, a "Spiritual MRI." She can offer you guidance as to where you are on the journey and what areas you want to examine more deeply to help things move along. Visit The 3rd Eye website for more information.

While some of the initial clearing work may seem harsh or difficult at first, a greater knowing within you will keep you moving forward, and you will truly understand the higher meaning of the guiding hand of Light. Because we have been through these stages already, we are always available to help you as you walk through the various doorways and gateways. The soundscapes are energetic breadcrumbs that we have sent you to pick up as needed. Each of our offerings has been carefully crafted to allow you the most full-spectrum engagement of the energy as is possible.

Consider one facet of what these soundscapes represent as being a kind of energetic food, or fuel. The energy of the music is absorbed through intent.

It may be important at times to back off the DNA soundscapes until you can integrate the information and content that has been released. We have various other soundscapes in our catalog that are there to assist you. The DNA LevelOne series is a full sonic encyclopedia set of a vast Sonic Mystery School. Each of the other soundscapes is a book or chapter taken out of the set to expand upon those teachings. We will share more about each of these other soundscapes in the back of the book.

A Greater Purpose

Ponder your life and your perception of the reality in which you live now. Do you believe that there is a greater intelligence overseeing life on this planet and the evolution of mankind? Would you agree that it is inherent in the fabric of our being to seek a higher order of existence, to continually strive to learn more and be more? If so, would you also concur that this Unified Intelligence/Source Vibration, out of which we all evolved, would have also created a means to communicate with this multidimensional existence of worlds within world. Following this stream of thought, this avenue of communication would need to bypass the ego mind and resonate at a cellular level of one's being in order to speak to and awaken the Expanded Self – the infinite aspect of one's nature that carries the memory and intelligence of many realms and existences. Sound/Music is the ideal carrier wave for this form of communication to occur – a direct Universal connection. Sonic transmissions from beyond the linear tick-tock world of 3D extending out to a world of energy, of Light and ultimately one that is abundant with possibilities of new creations. This is the 5th World of Light communicating with us.

Music is more than a gift of beauty and entertainment for mankind at this unparalleled moment in the Earth's history. It has been documented by science that certain resonant frequencies/sounds have profound effects on the codex within the DNA – keys that have been waiting for thousands, perhaps millions of years for the right evolutionary sequences and musical patterns to activate them. Your DNA accumulates all data, then sorts it and catalogs it constantly. It is your personal connection to what has been termed the Akashic Records, containing data from all of your incarnations, throughout all time and space. Learning how to tap into this wellspring of information will provide access to your personal potentials, but also to the unlimited source of Universal Intelligence – the Universal Energy Field (UEF).

It is not important that you personally know everything about everything (the task of that is immense), but what is important is that you know what you need to know right when you need to know it. This is Universal Intelligence, and you have within you the ability to tap into that unlimited Source and make the necessary connections to find the information you need to actualize the tasks and goals your heart desires. What this means to you is that once you set your intent on the tasks/goals/visions you want to manifest, you can put that desire out through the Universal communications system and tell the UEF just what you need. The music assists by providing the carrier wave of energy needed to send this directive out to ALL dimensional realms. Following this process, you can then become aware of how Spirit starts to bring forth the information/contacts/connections/information you need; this is the Law of Attraction in motion. You become a synchronicity generator. You increase your awareness of what is going on around you at all times and learn to interpret these clues and messages as they come to you. Learning when to act and when to observe are the skills you will learn as you go deeper into this process. You can do this without the music, but the music amplifies the energy and is able to penetrate spaces that you are not capable of accessing yet.

Consider one facet of what these soundscapes represent as a kind of energetic food, or fuel. The energy of the music is absorbed through intent. As an example, you decide you want to write a book, but you don't know anything about how to make that happen. So you set your intent and ask the UEF to provide you with the information you need to know to get you started. While listening to the music, you use your imagination and creativity to begin painting the picture of this reality. What you initially see first is the end result – that of being a successful author. But there are many steps that you will need to take before that happens. You set this goal and initiate the process to begin. This spark of desire is captured and literally goes out into the UEF and starts to make connections that match the energetic composition of that intent. That afternoon you go out to lunch with a friend, and she tells you that she just met this wonderful person who is an author and has just been published. She invites you to meet him for dinner that weekend at her house so you can talk to him about book publishing. This is synchronicity which can be generated daily in your life if you learn how to master this process consistently and continuously throughout your journey to manifesting your life as a published author. The more your DNA becomes activated, the quicker this all happens. Rather than spin your wheels doing the "work harder to succeed more" routine, you will learn to slow down, be still more and manifest by making a deeper connection to the Universal Energy Field and Source Vibration.

Energetic Transmissions of Information

Many things are changing in our daily world and with the accelerating consciousness on the planet, much will be revealed about individual purpose and the desire to step into our unique place of service. As the greater planetary matrix evolves into a higher vibrational state, we will be increasingly challenged to expand our individual consciousness to take on more and more information. The information age is truly upon us. We have developed the capability of our mental self to absorb, catalog and disseminate data using the standard models of curriculum development in our schools. It is now time to develop new techniques for absorbing data directly from the Universal Energy Field (UEF) in order to keep up with this evolving flow of information. But first we must learn to reign in the ego and quiet the chatter of the mind in order to develop this new ability.

These soundscapes can assist you in the process of obtaining information directly from the UEF – via osmosis. The greatest factors effecting the type of experience and benefits you will have from listening to these frequencies is your intent and your dominant desires. They will meet you wherever you are in your abilities and in your capacity to reach beyond the limitations, resistances and barriers of this 3D realm in which most people primarily exist. Setting aside time each day for this purpose, to develop this skill, is essential. Think of all the things that demand your time, energy and attention each day. It is safe to say the majority of what we do and give ourselves to is very much connected to our 3D reality. If you feel you are wanting to move forward with the evolutionary current, then we suggest you begin by committing to one hour minimum to that which is not of this world each day and then increase it from there.

Within each of us lives a source and vibration that is our Essence. This Essence is in need of our cooperation, participation and partnership. Once this connection is made, we get it; what we focus on grows, and our Spirit is just as much in need of our energetic attention as the ever-controlling ego that has dominion over the 3D world. The needs and desires of the ego are endless and it initially takes consistent awareness to transform your consciousness to focus on the spiritual reality.

The frequencies used in these soundscapes span throughout many dimensions and are comprised of inter-penetrating overlays in the subtlest realms of the UEF. Therefore, this is why we recommended that you use the highest quality sound system you can to benefit from these intricately profound vibrations. When you are doing a focused session, play the music at a higher volume than "just background" – you want to feel the music vibrating in your cells as much as possible. By using an external stereo system, the subtle vibrations will enhance the environment they are played in as well and assist you in expanding your awareness into the etheric layers of your multidimensional self, via the nadis and the chakra system. However, in order to quiet the mind, deepen your meditative practice and connect with the wisdom and guidance of your Higher Self's infinite wisdom, you must surrender the busy-ness of your 3D reality and ego chatter to an intentional and sacred space where you engage with the soundscapes each day. The more you do this, the quicker you will move forward on your path.

Evolutionary Sounds

We use evolutionary sounds to trigger the DNA codex to activate and evolve to a higher order of functioning. These are sound patterns and combinations that we create during deep shamanic states. Through focused intent, we extend our energetic reach to connect with Source Vibration and explore the Universal Energy Field (UEF). The more YOU reach out to IT, the more IT reaches back to YOU. We use computers, synths and sound design software to create our palette of sounds – a gifting of alien-based technology offered to humanity to awaken our higher potentials through multidimensional sound. It is an advanced form of communication that is established in order to finely attune our being to these frequencies. While some of the sounds you will hear are familiar to you, many of the sounds will not be. Once you establish resonance however, they will become very comforting to the aware conscious traveler.

Our intent is to unlock and activate the codex within the DNA through sound and vibration.

Music & Sound can be created to control and manipulate and has been used for that purpose in many ways throughout society. Music can move an entire generation or group of beings in to a certain direction in the vast consciousness field. We leave this for you to think about in the music of the past as well as the music that is being promoted now via the mass-marketing machines. We seek to break free of these limiting patterns and expand the frequency spectrum so that we can consciously choose where we want to explore and expand our realms of experience while here in a 3D form. The potentials are really unlimited and dependent on your willingness to step outside the predefined boxes of how you have been told to live your life.

The planet and all the beings that inhabit her are all a part of a vast Universe with an infinite intelligence and capacity for extending that wisdom and higher order of being to us. The desire and intent of this unified intelligence is Oneness versus separation. We have no agenda other than to offer one way of reaching a more illuminated capacity of who you are, knowing that as we empower others we, in turn, are empowered, and we all move up another rung of the evolutionary ladder. If you have a specific religion, you will find that energetic signature represented in the soundscapes, and so people often feel that we are receiving direct transmissions from a specific group soul. However, it is just sympathetic resonance connecting to what is already in them. Because of that strong sense of resonance, they assume that this is our experience or focus as well – It is Not.

During the initial 10 years of research as we were developing the work, many individuals came to our Odyssey Sound & Light Temple and brought with them the spiritual aspect of Source Vibration that they represented: Christian, Jewish, Muslim, Buddhism, Taoism, Hinduism, Jehovah's, starseed, indigo, crystals, alien, etc. All of these people left their energetic seeds for the highest visions for a peaceful, loving planet, and these were captured in the sounds as a way to share the ONEness of us all. We were given a data collector to capture this information in the form of a Lightbrary Cathedral Crystal, called Grandfather. He remains an ever present contributor to all of the projects we create. Our personal religion and philosophy is the LOVE of the Universe flowing through us – to surrender the ego-mind and get out of the way so that the power of that Love can activate the full capacity of our being in service to the unification and transformation of mankind.

The creation process for the DNA LevelOne series (1989-1996) was brought through in real time session with clients in the Odyssey Sound & Light Temple. JoAnn would do vibrational healing sessions while Gary played the sounds to accompany what was happening with the client. Several years were spent prior to this phase just on sound design alone, so that Gary would have the palette of sounds available, as he was guided during these live sessions to get out of the way as much as possible. There are no overdubs, no additional tracks added after the initial transmissions were received. They are instrumental soundtracks only, with no guided journeys, subliminals or verbal instructions on them.

If you have ever been to see a really good trance channel, you notice that the personality of the person moves out of the way so that the higher messages can come through without the filter of the personality. This process is similar with the exception that Gary must maintain focus on the technology as he must play the keys, move the mouse and open up sound libraries. His left and right brain have to work in totally harmony for this all to come through in the way that it does. This is the advanced levels of training that is required for him to do this work.

> *"This music is a gift from Source/God/All That Is, we are just channels for the divine spirit to flow through us to those ready to move to the next evolutionary step for humankind."*

The DNA 1.5 (2011) and the DNA.L2 (2006-2009) were created in a slightly different way than the LevelOne series. Rather than bring them through in a real time setting, they were received in packets of downloaded transmissions. Each one then seamlessly fits into the next. So they were still brought through while in deep shamanic states, but they were also composed using layers and various other techniques that Gary developed; he continues to evolve his musical creation process. There are voices of various kinds throughout these levels, with a few areas where words can be distinguished, but very little. Mostly the vocals tones are created for a certain effect designed to shift the assemblage point in a certain way as opposed to creating any kind of specific vocal message. JoAnn also lays in a vocal track of sound healing toning and chanting to add to the project once the compositions are completed. While evolutionary intent is found throughout all the soundscapes, there is never any underlying subliminal message placed directly into or under the sound. You may hear voices deep in the layers which are a shamanic style of toning, chanting and sound healing-style phrases. We also do not use any other sound technology under the music or alternate tunings in any way as it is not necessary with our QSET technique. Our sounds are very holographic in scope and reach all dimensional levels of the human bio-energetic field. The transmissions we receive are pure communications from the higher realms of Light – no editing allowed.

For Spiritual Seekers

Because we have been offering these soundscapes to the public since 2000, we have a good understanding of who can benefit the most from working with them. Using marketing terms, the demographic would be called "conscious evolutionaries, cultural creatives, starseeds, lightworkers in service, planetary healers, indigos, crystals, evolutionary agents of change, seekers of truth, anyone in higher service to humanity, etc." The age group is from pre-birth to final transition, with the predominant being 25-65 years old. As for gender, males are more interested in the 25-35 group and women in the 40-55 group.

Healers of all kinds are exploring this work first, and once they become familiar with the process, they are sharing them with their clients. The music is ideal for all massage and therapeutic type treatments. Psychologists and psychotherapists are using them for visualization, spiritual journeying, rebirthing, breathwork, regression and hypnosis. Dance and movement teachers are also finding them to be valuable in teaching more about connecting deeper to the bodies' subtle movements. Healing centers and wellness clinics are using them in the background for maintaining calmness and to create a peaceful energy in their environments. Anyone interested in altered states of consciousness, paranormal abilities, psychic awakening, advanced learning, brain/mind explorations, lucid dreaming, remove viewing, out of body experiences and those who love to explore the unknown are drawn to work with them.

There are a lot of people using them for psychedelic explorations and in conjunction with plant teachers. Because of the expanded consciousness state attained while engaging with these types of plant teachers or psychedelics, you will find the music to be an amazing visual landscape to explore during your shamanic journeys. Once you connect to a soundscape during an altered state, you will find that your unaltered shamanic journeying meditations will increase in power, and you will understand the potentials within these soundscapes even more.

As for us personally, we have engaged with many of the plant teachers and psychedelics in our early years. But for the last 20 years, we have not had any desire as our ability to attain an altered state with the music far surpasses our desire to engage in substances. We feel that at some point in your spiritual development journey, you can learn how to access these realms without substances. We still see them as great teaching tools and openers for the mind that perhaps could not be made any other way – especially those with rigid mental bodies that keep a tight grip on the narrow 3D reality. Without our early use, we would not be able to do what we do now. For the sake of you know who, we are not recommending it. Use with wise judgment and discernment if you choose to engage with our music while under the influence of any other substance. Don't underestimate the power of the music.

As for those who do not seem to resonate with this work, that would be people who are heavily invested in the mental realms of 3D reality, those of a more analytical, prove-it-to-me type of thinking. They will find that sinking down and letting go into this type of music to be annoying and irritating – probably discordant. The more one only sees black and white and not shades of gray, the less likely they will enjoy this type of adventure. Anyone who is in fear of the unknown will not be able to engage with this music, as it does call on you to go deeper into who you are, beyond the layers of fear and anxiety. Anyone with mental instability should not work with them, as it could enhance aspects of their consciousness that would create more confusion.

Often times, someone may start the soundscapes, and it brings up fears, so they put them away and come back again at a later time after they have done some other types of emotional clearing or processing work. They will then find them to be right in alignment with where they are. So if that happens with you, know that it is perfectly fine. When you are able to ease into them, you will truly know that you have evolved to another level of Light within your being, and it is time to celebrate the work you have done to get there.

Remember too, that we are always here to support you should you find that it is bringing up areas within your consciousness that you don't understand. Often we can offer simple guidance to get you through to the next level of the adventure.

Faith & Trust

Ultimately stepping into this work is about faith and trust in an unseen power that fills you with so much Love that it is undeniable to you that what you know in your heart is truth. For those considering DNA Activation as a part of their spiritual path, we encourage you to use discernment and to find that deep place within you that signifies this music is the right tool for you to use at this time. As for how we know that it is safe and that what is said in our writings and teachings about this process of DNA Activation is valid, is because we walk and talk this work in our lives every day. We are committed to doing the work first on ourselves and then sharing it with others as we receive direct confirmation that the alignments are in tune with the Multidimensional-Holographic Frequency Packets (MFPs) we received. We engage with others on a daily basis who are doing the same with consistently positive results.

We envision that humanity is so much more than what is currently the mainstream "normal." As we have attained various levels of self-empowerment, we know that we can move beyond the limitations that are presented and accepted as current truths. The body temple is capable of amazing things, and we know that we can access that through sound and conscious intent. We are fully capable of self-healing, rejuvenation and reversing aging and so much more. The body is Light, and while we currently hold dominance in a realm of density, we can still shift the assemblage point of our focus to a body that emanates Light all of the time. Light regenerates continuously, never dies, never deteriorates. This actualization can lead us to more conscious forms of living and transitioning to the next realms when we so choose. Death no longer has to be viewed the same; we can learn to ascend to the next plane of existence consciously when it is time for us to leave at our choosing. Many accept that we are immortal and go on even after our time here on Earth, yet they don't see that we can move through this in a much different way than it is currently being actualized. Being dis-eased in old age and dying will no longer be a part of life. These are some of the main focuses and directions of our personal work and explorations with this music, and we do this in the spirit of deep self-reflection and commitment.

As for what the DNA soundscapes have done for us personally, initially we were able to call forth many pastlives that contained dormant talents and gifts already learned that we were able to bring through and use at this time. We were also able to review our incarnational agreements to unfold the reason why we incarnated together in this timeline. Just one example: the concepts used in the Odyssey Sound & Light Temple emanated primarily from an Atlantean lifetime in which we were involved in similar healing work together using sound, crystals and energy healing. Our intuitive/psychic abilities surfaced quickly, which assisted us in our manifestation, abundance and development of our projects. An increase in intelligence allowed us to quickly learn the left-brained technology that was needed to bring all aspects of our work into tangible form in 3D. A clearing away of karmic ties and threads enabled us to move smoothly into doing our work full-time without the drag of emotional baggage pulling on us. During our first 10 years, we had "day" jobs, but since 2000, we have been able to hold the energy steady enough to ride the waves while having our 3D needs supported. Our personal relationship is what is termed Twin Flames, as we are as One, while we also maintain our unique individuality, which is encouraged and respected by each other. There is no emotional drama between us which keeps the energy at consistently higher levels. What we need to do our work is always there when it is time, and the gift of enjoying the journey is truly entrained in our every moment reality. These "walk your talk" manifestations tell us that these soundscapes truly are what they say they are. We could not offer these to you if we did not feel they were a valuable contributor to our life path and purpose.

We have explored the health and care of the physical body from many different angles. We do a raw living-food diet primarily and use various power foods to supplement the needs of a carbon body in transition to a light body. We do regular cleanses and detoxes to keep up with the pollutants from our environment and feel vital and healthy. We are most definitely healthier now than when we were in our 20s.

One of the main areas people like to know about is if one can be financially supported to do their spiritual work. As a collective society, we are currently in the beginnings of shifting from a 3D- based economy to a 5D one, which in itself is quite the challenge. Understanding abundance and how it works in the 5th World is so new to many that the old world concepts are constantly bumping into the new world ones. It is a dance one has to walk through and learn step by step. The ego-self and survival-self is very strong in its need to have things, while the

5D-self knows it has everything it needs in the moment. Much has to be examined as you step into this new reality.

Looking back over our personal journey, it was necessary for our development that we start the work with nothing. When we came together in 1988, we had nothing but strong visions and clear directions in our minds and hearts to work from. Many cannot imagine that one would be supported to be able to do their fullest expression of Light, but we knew that we had to. At that time, no one was talking about DNA Activation, so we knew we really had a challenge ahead of us. We were both willing to take the risks involved as well as make the sacrifices. Making a conscious choice to not have children helped us greatly in being able to push the comfort boundaries when we needed to. It has been expensive to keep up with the latest in sound development and recording technology, as our work/mission tends to always require more money to continue. Our basic needs are really minimal, but our global mission work does move us in the million+ dollar range. One must develop the energetic configuration to be able to wield this amount of energy in the form of money on this planet in this way. Holding true to 5th world principles is a whole new way of attaining financial wealth. It is significantly different than making money in the 3D world. It takes a lot of deep personal development to manifest money in alignment with walking a dedicated path of Light holding the highest levels of integrity in all interactions and agreements.

We have had many powerful and very significant influxes of money throughout our journey. They always seemed to have come at very crucial points within our spiritual development cycles. We would push the energy as far as we could and stand strong, sometimes during great difficulty to go the other way, and then something magical would happen and the money would appear. It is difficult to sit in that space of sometimes waiting for the energy configuration to align so that this can occur, and yet that is where trust and faith is truly developed. Giving in or selling out, as they would call it, is the direct affirmation you send back to the Universe when you cannot hold true to your inner compass, but you have to be wise in these decisions as well. Money has been gifted to us by unexpected sources many times including winning the Fantasy 5 lottery twice. These were both surrounded by magical circumstances in which the tickets were purchased, so we know that for us it was a direct message from Spirit to indicate that we must continue, and we were doing the right thing.

We have always had what we truly needed at all times even if it didn't appear that way to our 3D selves. All the lessons we have been through in relation to money have been important to our personal journeys. We are not entirely free of financial frustration, because we do have big visions that we feel we are here to accomplish which require large sums of money. When we stop and view it from the higher perspective, we can release the anxious feelings and accept the state of flow we are in at all times. We've always considered ourselves to be of the turtle clan as we move slowly and steadily along the path, building a strong foundation, mastering skills and maintaining the quality and integrity throughout all aspects of our business and personal lives. We are always available to talk to others about this work and feel that is important to the trust that you need when engaging in this type of deep spiritual work.

Things to Consider

In stepping into the unknown aspects of who you are and asking to be shown what has previously been hidden from your aware self, you are agreeing to the challenge of aligning your entire beingness with the higher potentials of your Soul Essence. That means that any part of your life or who you are in it that is not true to Spirit and the truth of who you are will be shaken up. We mean this figuratively and literally; the music will create new vibrational patterns within the neural system and the cellular levels of your being that will release informational content that is new to your awareness. The ego will not be content with this exposure and will act out with unusual and impulsive behaviors as you clearly decide to peel away the illusions, resistances, false personas and toxic relationships that are keeping you from your highest expressions of Light. It is not unusual for things in your reality to appear to get worse before getting better. Know that this a part of the process, and it only lasts as long as you decide it is necessary.

The DNA soundscapes will not make you sick or create chaos in your life in and of themselves, but they will make it increasingly difficult for you to hide your shadow self, as well as your Light. We are Light beings in our natural state, our Soul Level. It is our cultural conditioning that has contributed to the disconnect and isolation from our true essence; a fall from the state of grace. It is the continuation of habitual patterns, addictions and unresolved emotions that contributes to the dis-ease process in the body. Self-healing becomes a primary area of focus and concern as you continue the clearing and releasing process. All that is of Light within us is an encoded frequency packet within our DNA codex. To access this intelligence we must go through and face all those things that alienated us from Source Vibration and the awareness of our Oneness. Without fully knowing our darkness, we cannot fully embrace our full expression of Light.

All of our life experiences have been a necessary journey for a Soul to travel along the path of ascension to each successive new realm of awareness. None of the experiences you have engaged with have been unnecessary to your overall evolutionary adventures. If there is dis-ease currently in your body, you can use the frequencies in these soundscapes to discover how that program was created and why. While we do not make medical claims or encourage foregoing medical treatment, we believe in the body's ability to heal itself and in the process of ingesting certain harmonic frequencies to re-establish balance where the body has otherwise learned to compensate for dis-harmony. This is a journey that each individual must decide upon for themselves. Each person's experience will be different because we are all at a very unique place on our evolutionary spiritual journey. You must be very clear that your alignment with your unique expression is what you truly want above all else. Once that intent is activated, the DNA soundscapes will empower you to find your way and will work continuously to provide you with the release of information to reveal the guidance you need right when you need it.

As we have already implied, DNA Activation is not recommended if you are in an emotionally unstable or depressed state, as it can emphasize these emotions further. With that said, once you have reached a level of spiritual development where you clearly understand the powerful information that can be found within a deep dive into fear-filled or depressed energy, then you will find the music to be a profound therapist and teacher in helping you to transform that energy to empower you. If you are dealing with serious mental illness, this work is not recommended for you at this time as it could further enhance delusional states. We do have other soundscapes that will assist in your healing process and would be happy to assist you in alternative listening to get you back to a more centered place before beginning the DNA Activation adventure.

It is not possible for harm or anything dark to be connected to these soundscapes. We have placed protections within them to assure the Light always prevails. They come from a very pure and immensely loving intent that wants nothing more than for you to shine your brightest Light to the World. Children, pets, even plants have a tendency to respond very positively to these sounds, perhaps because they have less resistance, less judgment and more clarity in their perception of reality. With that said, those who may carry darkness in their field will have resistance and that could cause outward reactions of a negative vibration to occur. Just be aware and sensitive to those around you and use good judgment as to when to play them in your spaces. Don't assume just because you are loving them and engaged with the sounds that it will be the same for others around you.

The "work" of DNA Activation begins with your intent and thus ultimately with your agreement and consent. Having them on in your environment will not have adverse effects on casual listeners. Their experience will be very different from yours because you have agreed to the "work." You will also come to understand that as you do things that are in alignment with your highest good, it will also be for the highest good of those around you. This may not always present itself in a positive outward manifestation at first, but in time, it will be shown to have been what everyone needed to grow and evolve their Light. As you engage with the resistances that emerge from the personal changes you need to make, you will continually be challenged to hold a higher state at all times amidst these challenges. This is part of the spiritual development process, and it becomes easier as you continue to walk your path of truth above all else. Learning to share from your heart centered space is a necessary skill you will learn in order to share the Light you have emerging within you. This in turn will open the hearts and minds of those around you.

Sonic Mystery School

This is a term that came to us as we explored diving deeply into these soundscapes more and more. The depth and expanse that we have experienced is quite profound and seemingly never ending. As many hours as we have explored them, we find them to be a continual treasure of amazing and magical adventures. One day it was clear we were creating this wonderful mystery school full of sonic information that only when the person was at the right evolutionary stage on their journey, would that information be released. Most mystery schools hold back information from the initiate based on someones personal judgment or initiations to determine when you are ready. The beauty of this mystery school is that it is always up to you and no one has the ability to make that decision for you. There is no one to blame or judge for holding you back, as only you can hold yourself back. Ultimately no more control structure determining your life path & purpose. No more Soul Contracts – think about the implications of that!

We also created the term, DNAvatar, to represent those who were really dedicated to the unfolding adventure of discovering what is possible by focusing time and attention on consciously shifting their DNA in alignment with their intent. This is also a chosen path that one walks when they truly feel they are here to embody the concepts within this vast body of work.

As you learn how to tap into the informational content within the soundscapes, you start to understand how profound this is on so many levels. We don't have anything for you to join or agendas that you are required to complete to be a DNAvatar and to be part of this Sonic Mystery School. Once you feel in alignment with that, you can register with us so that we can send you special communications from time to time related to being a flameholder for this work on the planet.

Explorations with Other Soundscapes

In addition to the DNA Activation LevelOne, 1.5 and L2 series, we also have many other soundscapes in our catalog that we strongly suggest you engage with as well. As stated before these other soundscapes are chapters or books taken out of the overall DNA sonic encyclopedia series and expanded upon. We will share a little bit about each one so you understand what we mean.

Our Healing soundscape is a great place for beginners to start as it is loving and gentle. It guides you into deep spaces but doesn't push the flow. This one is great to use at times when you feel you need a rest or a break, especially during times when the physical body needs to detox or purge. It is the most gentle one we offer.

The Odyssey soundscape was designed to balance the chakras, expand the auric field and ground your energy in preparation for the DNA Activation work. It is great to use anytime you start to feel really off balance in your life. Use it along with a guided journey we offer to learn the best technique for balancing your chakras.

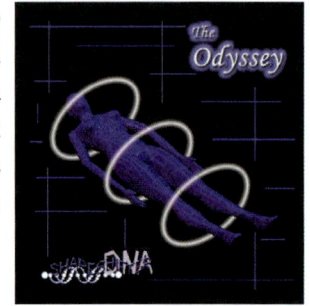

The Shamballa soundscape is for when you are connecting with the higher realms of ascended masters and want to connect with your

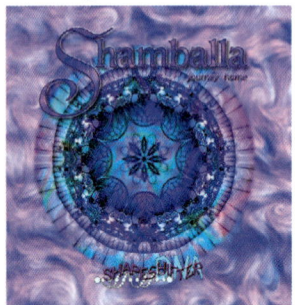

guidance teams. It is a very deep and expansive soundscape and often puts you to sleep easily at first. In time, it can take you deep into theta states and eventually into holding consciousness in a delta state. It is aligned with the ascended masters in the Shamballa Temples.

ReJuva works a lot on rejuvenating the body temple and touching you into your higher states of joy and playfulness, bringing out the happy creative child within the serious adult form. It is filled with water-based resonant frequencies, so it really helps to purify and cleanse the physical body temple – ReJuvenation.

Sanctuary is a treasure of comfort and peace amidst a seemingly chaotic world. This soundscapes connects you with the elemental realms and assists you in building the bridges to the 5th World. This is another one that is great when you feel you just need a place to rest and be still.

Our Transmissions of Light Codes (TLC) series was created from our live concerts featuring some sound healing and chanting vocals. Aya's Underworld is for deeper explorations into your shadow realms – diving into the underworld to gain in strength and power.

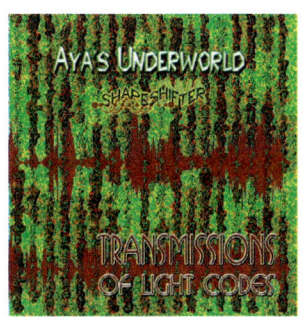

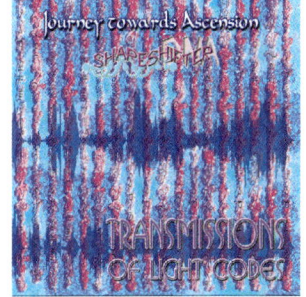

Journey towards Ascension helps to gradually build the bridges between dimensional realms and to pierce the veils into many doorways of evolutionary potentials. Great to work with for serious ascension work.

5th World Emerging is a joy-filled piece to help you shift your perspective to living life in these higher realms. Etheric templates are presented to help you build the architecture of your new world of light manifested.

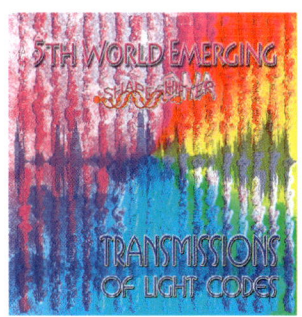

Journey of the Soul is an amazing deep journey taking you through all your incarnations into this current one, allowing you to explore the patterns you have been bringing forth with each new incarnation.

We also suggest you take our pre-recorded webinars and practice the guided journeys in the Activate Your DNA DVD series – #1 and #2. These will help you to initially learn how to build your spiritual foundation and to work more effectively with the music.

A Visual Journey

We will leave you with some imagery to help you begin to see a more expanded vision of engaging with this body of Sound. Imagine a vast and loving gathering of extraordinary Beings of Light representing many dimensions who have evolved beyond us. Each Being embodies great wisdom and knowledge from eons of advanced spiritual development. They have gathered together for the purpose of assisting mankind to shift into its Universal expansion and evolution. When you put on #1 of the DNA Activation soundscapes, one of these vast Beings steps up and extends the vibrational frequency of its Being out through the ethers, onto Planet Earth and through the portal of data streams (Multidimensional-Holographic Frequency Packets/MFPs) in these soundscapes. As this profound energy exchange is connecting with you, all the other Ascended Beings of light stand in support of your desire to consciously evolve to the next higher levels of your incarnational cycles. They each extend their own essence through the 1st Being of Light, but from a more diluted place of influence, so as not to overwhelm your neural system. In your mind's eye, see them standing one behind the other with their arms extended on the shoulder of those before them, their influence and wisdom pulsing through and in support of the Light Being called upon in that moment. As you absorb the transmissions your body is able to receive in the beginning stages of awakening your dormant potentials, you are in effect, already being prepared for increased awareness and a higher vibration of frequency.

With each new soundscape, Ascended Master energy is offered to you to prepare the body temple to increase your Light Quotient. When you listen to #2, the Being you have been working with in #1 steps back and the Being of #2 steps up – offering a subtle but profound heightening of frequencies, all the while interfacing and being influenced by a predominant spectrum of frequency from each of these loving and infinite Beings. With each soundscape, the vortex of power and energy of influence increases as does your capacity to accrete more light and assimilate greater levels of vibration, grounding the influence of these loving and wise Beings throughout many dimensions into your everyday self. The soundscapes will illuminate frequency bands for you so that you can work on appropriate areas of your life in order to come to a balanced state of consciousness. All the soundscapes in our catalog are building the multidimensional frequency maps to allow you to gracefully explore these spaces – creating a smoother transition process from 3D to 5D Reality Constructs.

As we evolve, both individually and as a species, we gradually increase our Light Quotient to be able to exist within the more rarefied dimensional realms of reality. When you see the phrase "Lighten Up," you will now know that is a literal statement of intent. We primarily exist in the 3rd dimension as carbon based physical bodies of flesh, bone and blood, but we are evolving to hold our focus and attention in the 5th World of Light and will gradually exist within a body of pure light; this is the ascension process. All this is actualized in a timeline in which you can assimilate the changes more easily and quickly by using this music as a guide. This is ultimately what the true gift of these soundscapes are for – to help you shapeshift throughout this process.

Enjoy your Journeys.

About Us

Rather than repeat this info for those interested, you can refer to the first book in this series for our bios – Sound, Light & Frequency. You can also download a more lengthy bio on our website.

ActivateYourDNA.com/about.html

Closing

In closing, we want to share that this book is a place to start your DNA Activation journey. We plan to continue this series by expanding on many of the thought streams we already started here. We also want you to share your thoughts and experiences with us to help guide the flow of information. You can email us or engage with our Blog to share thoughts and ideas with others.We are on this journey together and our collective desire to evolve consciously is a collaborate adventure. Welcome to the Journey.

Gary & JoAnn Chambers

Gratitude & Thanks

We want to extend our gratitude to Dielle Ciesco for her help in editing this book and being a supportive Light of our work over the years. Dielle's beautiful voice is featured in our TLC soundscape series, and she has assisted us in developing teaching materials and webinars. She is a DNAvatar and has been working with the DNA Activation soundscapes since 2004. She is also the author of two wonderful books on the power of sound, words, and voice which we recommend you check out.

Visit Dielle at DielleCiesco.com.

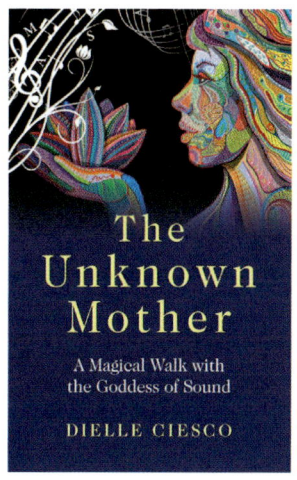

Free MP3 Music Soundfile

Get started by listening to your first sample of our DNA Activation LevelOne soundscapes. This is the first 10 minutes from the #1 track which will give you a great starting point from which to begin your adventures.

ActivateYourDNA.com/download/freeDownload.html

Then spend some time visiting our main website and listening to sample soundfiles and get started with your first soundscape.

VisionaryMusic.com

Printed in Great Britain
by Amazon